New Curriculum

Primary English

Learn, practise and revise

Les Ray and Gill Budgell

Year **4**

Contents

RISING STARS

Content grid

Links to English Programme of Study for Key Stage 2

	Unit title	Objective	Focus	Speak about it
1	Homophones	Homophones or near-homophones	Word reading, spelling and word structure	Terminology: homophones Purpose and links to spelling and meaning
2	Sounds and letters	Words with the /ei/ sound spelled -ei, -eigh, or -ey	Word reading, spelling and word structure	Exploring different spellings of phonemes
3	Forms of poetry: ballads	Recognise some different forms of poetry (e.g. free verse, narrative poetry)	Comprehension, composition and text structure	Compare how a common theme is presented in poetry, prose and media
4	Adding suffixes beginning with vowels	Add suffixes beginning with vowel letters to words of more than one syllable	Word reading, spelling and word structure	Terminology: suffixes Purpose and links to spelling and meaning
5	Investigating non-fiction	In non-narrative material, use simple organisational devices such as headings and sub-headings; retrieve and record information from non-fiction	Comprehension, composition and text structure	Purpose, audience and text features
6	Punctuation of direct speech	Use and punctuate direct speech	Composition and punctuation	Characters and speech
7	Test your grammar, punctuation and spelling	• Nouns and pronouns • Inverted commas (speech marks) • Adding suffixes beginning with vowels to words of more than one syllable • Sound /i/ spelled with a *y* within words		
8	Creating characters	In narratives, create settings, characters and plot	Comprehension, composition and text structure	Characters and characterisation
9	Words from other countries	Words with the /k/ sound spelled ch- (Greek in origin); words with the /sh/ sound spelled ch- (mostly French in origin); words ending with the /g/ sound spelled -gue and the /k/ sound spelled -que (French in origin); words with the /s/ sound spelled sc- (Latin in origin)	Word reading, spelling and word structure	Research skills
10	Similes	Discuss words and phrases that capture the reader's interest and imagination	Comprehension and composition	Terminology: similes
11	Metaphors	Discuss words and phrases that capture the reader's interest and imagination	Comprehension and composition	Terminology: metaphors Purpose and audience
12	Creating settings: suspense	In narratives, create settings, characters and plot	Composition and text structure	Terminology: suspense Personal experiences and opinions
13	Genre: westerns	Identify themes and conventions in a wide range of books	Comprehension, composition and text structure	Personal experience of different media Text features
14	Test your grammar, punctuation and spelling	• Verb inflections and Standard English • Fronted adverbials • Plural *s* and possessive *s* • Spelling common words • Sound /u/ spelled as -ou		

	Unit title	Objective	Focus	Speak about it
15	Genre: science fiction	Identify themes and conventions in a wide range of books	Comprehension, composition and text structure	Personal experience of different media Text features
16	Presenting poetry	Prepare poems and playscripts to read aloud and to perform, showing understanding through intonation, tone, volume and action	Comprehension, composition and text structure	Exploring a poem
17	Suffixes – the 'shun' sound	The suffix -tion is added to verbs to form nouns	Word reading, spelling and word structure	Suffix – /shun/
18	Explanations	Identify themes and conventions in a wide range of books	Comprehension, composition and text structure	Key text features and purpose
19	Advertisements	Identify themes and conventions in a wide range of books	Comprehension, composition and text structure	Key text features and purpose
20	Reading and interpreting playscripts	Prepare poems and playscripts to read aloud and to perform, showing understanding through intonation, tone, volume and action	Comprehension, composition and text structure	Personal experience of drama and humour
21	Test your grammar, punctuation and spelling	• Nouns and pronouns to avoid confusion across sentences • Apostrophes for plurals and possession • Commas before fronted adverbials • Suffix -ation • Commonly misspelled words		
22	Organising ideas around a theme	Identify main ideas drawn from more than one paragraph and summarise these; organise paragraphs around a theme	Word reading, spelling and text structure	Terminology, usage, purpose and effect
23	Standard English	Pupils should start to learn about some of the differences between Standard English and non-standard English and begin to apply what they have learned, for example in writing dialogue for characters	Word reading, spelling and word structure	Standard English
24	Pronouns	Choose nouns or pronouns appropriately within a sentence to avoid ambiguity and repetition; choose nouns or pronouns appropriately for clarity and cohesion	Composition, sentence structure, text structure	Pronouns
25	Commas to mark clauses	Use fronted adverbials; use commas after fronted adverbials	Comprehension, composition, sentence structure and punctuation	Terminology, usage, purpose and effect
26	Time and cause	Use conjunctions, adverbs and prepositions to express time and cause	Composition, sentence structure and text structure	Terminology, usage, purpose and effect
27	Apostrophes for possession	Indicate possession by using the possessive apostrophe with singular and plural nouns	Word structure, punctuation	Terminology, usage, purpose and effect
28	Test your grammar, punctuation and spelling	• Personal pronouns, possessive pronouns and adverbials • Verb inflections • Commas with fronted adverbials • Common words • Suffix /shun/		

1 Homophones

What happens when words sound the same but have very different meanings or spellings? Let's investigate!

Alice follows a white rabbit, falls through a hole in the ground and finds herself in a very strange world.

Here she meets a peculiar mouse.

From *Alice in Wonderland*

"You promised to tell me your history, you know," said Alice, "and why it is you hate – C and D," she added in a whisper, half afraid that it would be offended again.

"Mine is a long and sad tale!" said the Mouse, turning to Alice and sighing.

"It is a long tail certainly," said Alice, looking down with wonder at the Mouse's tail; "but why do you call it sad?" And she kept puzzling about it while the Mouse was speaking, so that her idea of the tale was something like this ...

Lewis Carroll

A Long Tale

Fury said to
  A mouse, That
    he met
     in the
     house,
      'Let us
      both go
     to law:
    I will
   prosecute
  you. –
  Come, I'll
   take no
    denial;
     We must
      have a
       trial:
        For
      really
     this
     morning
      I've
     nothing
    to do.'
   Said the
   Mouse to
  the cur,
  'Such a
   trial
   dear sir,
  With no
 jury or
judge,
  would be
  wasting
   our breath.'
    'I'll be
    judge,
   I'll be
   jury,'
 Said
  cunning
   Old Fury;
    'I'll try
     the whole
      cause,
     and
    condemn
     you
      to
       death.'

Speak about it

What is a **homophone**?
How are homophones different from words that sound the same?
Do you have any tricks to help you to spell them correctly?

Comprehension

1) How do we know that Alice was trying not to offend the mouse?

2) Which words tell us that the mouse is not very happy?

3) What do you notice about the story imagined by Alice?

4) Why does Alice say, "It is a long tail"?

5) How does this help us to understand what a homophone is?

6) Explain what is happening in the 'tail' poem?

7) Alice does not think the story is sad. What do you think? Give your reasons.

 Language focus

1) Find homophones for these words.

   a. grate   **b.** groan   **c.** here   **d.** knot   **e.** mail   **f.** main

2) Find homophones for these words. Use your dictionary to help.

   a. accept   **b.** affect   **c.** ball   **d.** berry   **e.** brake   **f.** fair
   g. meat   **h.** meddle   **i.** mist   **j.** peace   **k.** plane   **l.** scene

   Use them in sentences to show that you know the difference between them.

3) Write sentences to show the differences between the homophones in the words in 1) and 2).

4) These words each have one or more homophones. What are they?

   a. there   **b.** two   **c.** pair   **d.** heel   **e.** road   **f.** for

   Use them in sentences to show that you know the differences between them.

 Links to writing

1) Write a story about the confusion caused when someone writes the wrong homophone, e.g. supposing someone responded to this advertisement: 'Wanted – man who deals with leeks'. What kind of person might apply for the job? What kind of person might someone really be looking for?

2) Use the computer to make a glossary of homophones. Decide what makes a good glossary and how you will collect and organise the words. Use pictures to help make clear the differences between the words. Give some advice about how you can remember to spell the words correctly in the right context.

2 Sounds and letters

Some words contain different letters that make the same sound (or phoneme).
Let's investigate one sound – it is usually spelled -ai **as in the words** pain **and** rail.

I was **eight** years old before I stopped believing

> This uses **-eigh** to make the sound.

that at Christmas I would be given the chance

> This uses **-ei** to make the sound.

to see Rudolph the red-nosed **reindeer** and

> This uses **-ey** to make the sound.

his animal friends. **They** would be pulling Santa's

> This uses **-ei** to make the sound.

sleigh, with the red-coated jolly man at the **reins**.

> This uses **-eigh** to make the sound.

Every **day** leading up to Christmas I wouldn't **fail**

> This uses **-ay** to make the sound.

to climb out of bed, stare out of the window and

> This uses **-ai** to make the sound.

sigh at the empty skies. I could not **convey**

my sadness.

> This uses **-ey** to make the sound.

Here are some other examples.

-ai	-ei	-eigh	-ey	-ay
snail	vein	neighbour	grey	spray
tail	veil	freight	prey	stay
wail	reign	weight	obey	stray

Speak about it

How many different letter combinations on the page make the **-ai** sound?
What are they?
Look at where these letter combinations are found in the words. Can you make a rule?
Can you think of any other words to add to the columns in the chart?

Comprehension

1) How old was the writer in the passage?

2) What do reindeer traditionally do at Christmas?

3) What would Santa be doing with the reins?

4) Why do you think the writer sighed when he looked out of the window?

5) Do you think that the writer still believes in the reindeer?

Language focus

1) Write the correct **-ai** sounding word in these sentences.

   a.   Santa's _____ is pulled by reindeer.

   b.   I heard the horse _____ in the stable.

   c.   Half of sixteen is _____.

   d.   To take blood, the nurse looked for the _____ in his arm.

   e.   The lion _____ on smaller animals.

   f.   Scales are used to check _____.

   g.   The _____ was loaded onto the barge so it could be taken overseas.

2) Look at the **-ai** sounding words in the box.

   | grey   prey   they   obey   convey   survey |

   Where does the sound occur in the word? How is this different from words such as **pain**, **stain** and **remain**? Can you make a rule to help in spelling?

   Add a few more words with the same letters making the sound. Does the rule still work?

3) Which of the following words are not spelled correctly? Check in a dictionary.
   Write them correctly in sentences to show their meaning.

   veil   sprey   sheikh   reign   vien   obay   surveigh

Links to writing

1) Of course, words that make the **-ai** sound rhyme, even if they are not spelled the same.
   You could write an amusing poem. Use the following pattern. Check your rhymes in a
   dictionary.

Imagine a *vein*	Imagine a ...
As wide **as** a *drain*.	As ... as a ...
Imagine some *prey*	
As yellow **as** *hay*.	

3 Forms of poetry: ballads

How Comes that Blood? A ballad

'How comes that blood all over your shirt?
My son, come tell to me.'
'It's the blood of my good and friendly horse –
O mother, please let me be.'

'Your horse's blood is not so red.
My son, come tell to me.'
'It's the blood of my little hunting dog
That played in the field with me …'

'Your dog lies over there my son,
And this it could not be.'
'It is the blood of my old strong ox
That pulled the plough for me.'

'How comes the blood all over your shirt?
My son, you must tell to me.'
'It's the blood of my little brother Bill
Who I killed in the field today …'

'And what will you do when your father comes home?
My son, come tell it to me.'
'I'll put my feet in the bottom of a boat
And sail across the sea.'

Anon

Speak about it

A ballad is a story poem, originally meant to be sung. Are there any clues in the poem to prove this?
Stories should have a beginning, a developed middle and an end. Does it make any difference that this is a poem?
What do you find more difficult about reading the story in the form of a poem?
Think of other examples of texts that have the same theme, e.g. death, but aren't poetry such as non-fiction, film, play …

Comprehension

1) Who are the two characters speaking in this poem? How do you know?

2) What is the story really about?

3) What kind of excuses does the son give?

4) How do we know that his mother does not believe him?

5) Why do you think the son wants to be 'let be'?

6) Whose blood is on his shirt? Why is he telling so many lies?

7) Does the ending come as a shock? Why?

8) How does this story end? What does he have to do before his father returns?

Language focus

1) List what happens in each of the five verses of the poem.

2) What sort of pattern can you see in the way that the story is written?

3) Which verses would you say contain the beginning, the middle and the end of the story?

4) Tell the story of the first verse of the poem only. How can you make more of the setting, the characters and what they say and do?

5) How does the story build up to the tense moment when the son tells his mother what he did?

Links to writing

1) Write the story in a different way, so that the ending is different, as if it is true that the blood is from the boy's horse. Think about how he could prove his mother wrong every time she questions him.

2) What would happen if the boy stayed to meet his father? Continue the story and explain how and why he killed his brother.

3) Write paragraphs using a computer. Split up your lines to make it look like a poem. What difference does it make to the telling of the story?

4) Find some more old ballads using the Internet. Look at the stories they contain and see how they end.

4 Adding suffixes beginning with vowels

From *Flint*

He came right up close. "You're taking this one." He slammed the ball hard into Flint's stomach. "Nice and high, dropping for the far post. I'll be running in."

Marcus was in the crowded goal mouth with Chris and André and half a dozen Hammers. Rich hurried towards the far side, watched keenly by his marker.

Flint measured his strides back from the ball and took a slow steadying breath. *When had he last taken a corner?* Too long ago.

He ran. As his foot made contact, he knew it was good. The ball climbed as it crossed. Players jumped in procession, but the ball remained tantalizingly out of reach. Flint chased in.

Rich was running. The ball dropped, perfect for him, just in front of the far post. He dived.

Hurling himself sideways, the giant keeper stretched a finger to the ball.

As Rich and the keeper collided, Flint tore into the six-yard box. The ball was still floating in the goal mouth.

Defenders flailed and dived. Attackers pushed and collided. Somewhere in the midst of the mad scramble, a falling Hammer volleyed from the line.

Flint flung himself, head first, at the outcoming missile. The ball cannoned straight back on target. And this time there was no-one to block.

Neil Arksey

Speak about it

What is a suffix? Where does it come in a word?
Find examples in the passage. Are they all verbs?
Does the spelling of a word always change when you add a suffix?
Find examples in the passage.
Does it make any difference if the word you are adding it to has more than one syllable?
Are there any rules that can help you to spell the words correctly?

Comprehension

1) What advice does the player give Flint about taking the penalty?

2) How do you know there were lots of players protecting the goal?

3) Explain what Flint did to prepare for taking his shot.

4) What enables Flint to move into the six-yard box?

5) Quote the words to prove that there was great confusion around the goal mouth.

6) Which words tell you the force with which Flint and the ball moved towards the goal?

Language focus

1) Find all verbs in the passage. What happens to the spelling when you add a suffix that begins with a vowel? Write them in a chart like this.

Verb	Yesterday I …	I was …
to slam	slammed	slamming

2) Investigate the spelling of verbs when you change the tense. Write the following in your chart.

to garden   to limit   to begin   to forget   to prefer

Check your answers in a dictionary. Can you find a rule for these words of more than one syllable?

3) What happens if your verb ends in -e? Add the suffixes **-ed** and **-ing** to these words. Write the correct versions of these words in sentences.

to measure   to describe   to collide   to scramble   to pursue

4) What happens if your verb ends in -y? Add the suffixes **-ed** and **-ing** to these words. Write the correct versions of these words in sentences.

to hurry   to rely   to justify   to supply   to marry

Links to writing

1) Say these words: **to garden   to limit   to begin   to forget   to prefer**

Which part of the word do you stress most? **gar**den   gar**den**   **for**get   for**get**

Does the word end with one consonant letter?   garde**n**   forge**t**

Does that letter have a vowel in front of it?   gard**e**n   forg**e**t

Which words in the list double their last letter? Check in a dictionary.

Can you invent a rule?

5 Investigating non-fiction

London

Basic facts

London is the capital city of the United Kingdom. It covers approximately 1600 km² and has a population of over nine million people. London is the largest city in the UK.

The city was founded by the Romans as Londinium in AD43. It was situated on a terrace near the north bank of the river Thames. The Thames is tidal, and so London has been a convenient port since this time.

London has mild winters (an average of 6°C) in January. Summers are not known to be very hot, with an average of 21°C. The average rainfall is 600 mm. This is heaviest in the autumn months.

What to see in London

London is packed with things to see and do – and it's all too easy to miss things.

Museums

National museums in London are usually free. In the Natural History Museum are the skeletons of dinosaurs. Tate Britain and Tate Modern show the national collection of British paintings from the 16th century to today. Older paintings are held in the National Gallery.

Historic buildings

Everywhere in London are famous buildings reflecting the history of the city: the Tower of London, the Houses of Parliament, Guild Hall.

Entertainment

Theatres, and cinemas, can be found in Leicester Square and Shaftesbury Avenue in the West End. Shakespeare's Globe theatre is on the south bank of the Thames. To get away from the crowds, visit any of London's parks such as Hyde Park and Regent's Park.

So, whatever the weather, make sure that you plan your day in London to make the most of your visit.

Speak about it

What is the purpose of this piece of writing?

How do you know that it is non-fiction?

Where would you find this kind of writing?

Would you write in this style in school? If so, in which subjects?

Is it easy to get the information from it?

How do the headings, sub-headings and colours help?

Comprehension

1) How large is London in area and how many people live there?

2) Who founded the city? How can you tell from the use of its original name?

3) Which river runs through the city?

4) Where can you see the best collection of modern art?

5) Where would you go if you wanted to see dinosaur skeletons?

6) Where is Shakespeare's Globe theatre to be found?

Language focus

1) How easy is it to collect information from the passage? Use a chart.

Facts about London	What to see in London

Which features in the passage make it easier to collect information?

How do these features make this passage different from a description of London in a story?

2) Which topics does the writer use to help organise his/her work?

3) Write the sentences you would use to introduce each paragraph if you did not use sub-headings. What difference does this make?

4) Produce **an index** for this passage to help people find the information more easily.

   Find an index in another non-fiction book. What does it do? What does it look like?

   Pick out the most important points. The chart above will help.

   Put the points in alphabetical order.

   Write these in a list.

Links to writing

1) Write an account of an animal you have studied in class.

   How do you house it? What do you feed it?

   What is important to remember when looking after it?

   Use some of the features in the passage, e.g. **sub-headings**, **pictures**, to make your work easier to read.

2) Write a non-fiction piece about a place that you have visited on holiday.

   Decide which place and then list what makes it interesting.

6 Punctuation of direct speech

From *The BFG*

The Big Friendly Giant (BFG) has kidnapped Sophie.

Back in the cave, the Big Friendly Giant sat Sophie down once again on the enormous table. 'Is you quite snugly there in your nightie?' he asked. 'You isn't fridgy cold?'

'I'm fine,' Sophie said.

'I cannot help thinking,' said the BFG, 'about your poor mother and father. By now they must be jipping and skumping all over the house shouting "Hello hello where is Sophie gone?"'

'I don't have a mother and father,' Sophie said. 'They both died when I was a baby.'

'Oh, you poor little scrumplet!' cried the BFG. 'Is you not missing them very badly?'

'Not really,' Sophie said, 'because I never knew them.'

'You is making me sad,' the BFG said, rubbing his eyes.

'Don't be sad,' Sophie said. 'No one is going to be worrying too much about me. That place you took me from was the village orphanage. We are all orphans in there.'

'You is a norphan?'

Roald Dahl

Speak about it

What sort of character do you expect a giant to be?
How is the BFG different from other giants you have read about?
What is strange about the way he speaks?
Can you understand the words he uses? How?
The author writes down what the characters say to each other. What punctuation does he use?
Why does he put each new speaker on a new line?

Comprehension

1) What does the BFG's name tell you about his character?

2) Collect three examples from the passage to show that the BFG is kind.

3) Where does the giant live?

4) Where did he take Sophie from?

5) What is he most concerned about?

6) What happened to Sophie's parents?

7) Why does she not miss them?

Language focus

1) Punctuate the following direct speech from the passage.

   a. Is you quite snugly there in your nightie? he asked. You isn't fridgy cold?

   Note where the author uses speech marks and other punctuation.

2) Now punctuate the following using the same rules.

   a. Are you ready to go? she asked

   b. Certainly not, Ellie replied

   c. But you said to come at four o'clock, Jamal said

   d. That's not what I said at all, Mum shouted

   e. How nice to see you. Are you hungry? I said

3) In these examples more than one person is speaking. How do we have to set this out on the page? Look at the passage to see what Roald Dahl does.

   a. Now then said the policeman What's going on here? What a silly question replied the workman Can't you see we're digging a hole.

   b. What will you give me for a ride on my new bike? Tony asked A pound? A pound? Not likely Fred replied.

Links to writing

1) Write about what happens next. Write the speech in the same way to make the BFG likeable.

   Use speech marks.

   Put each new speaker on a new line.

   Put all the punctuation inside the speech marks.

7 Test your grammar, punctuation and spelling

Nouns and pronouns

Replace the underlined noun with a pronoun to avoid repetition within each sentence.

1) Paul is travelling to the seaside and <u>Paul</u> is excited.

2) Sal and Jen are on the train and <u>Sal and Jen</u> are excited to be going on holiday.

3) Joe gave <u>Joe's</u> sister a book to read.

4) Evie and Ellen waved goodbye to <u>Evie and Ellen's</u> parents.

5) The parents waved back and <u>the parents</u> felt a bit worried.

6) Paul and I found our seats and <u>Paul and I</u> settled down for the journey ahead.

Replacing pronouns with nouns

Replace the underlined pronoun with a noun to avoid confusion within each sentence.

1) They looked at the sheep out of the window and <u>they</u> laughed.

2) Peter took the apple out of the bag and weighed <u>it</u>.

3) The boys got their cards out and <u>they</u> began to perform tricks.

4) The girls opened their snack bags and <u>they</u> jumped about.

5) The dog chased the ball into the road and kicked <u>it</u>.

Inverted commas (speech marks)

Rewrite this passage correctly. Make sure each new speaker is on a new line and the inverted commas are in the correct places.

> We landed in a faraway place beyond the desert. It's quite magical I gasped.
> Is that all you can say about this mess we have got ourselves into? Oz replied.
> Well, it is … quite magical. It could be a lot worse! I replied. It could NOT be
> worse! We are lost like two aliens in the universe yelled Oz. I think he was angry,
> but I knew I was right and we'd be fine. I just needed time to show him.

Spelling

Adding suffixes beginning with vowels to words of more than one syllable

Add the suffix **-ing** to these words and make spelling adjustments to the new word if necessary.

Example   forget → forgetting

1) prefer

2) begin

3) garden

4) limit

5) travel

6) enrol

The sound /i/ spelled with a *y* within words

Solve the riddles. All the answers have a letter *y* sounding like /i/ in them.

1) A type of traditional story: m _ _ _

2) A country in Africa: E g _ _ _

3) A sport involving the performance of exercises requiring physical strength, flexibility, power, agility, coordination and balance: g _ _ n _ _ _ _ c _

4) A structure with triangular surfaces: p _ _ _ m _ _

5) Like a puzzle or a secret: m _ s t _ _ _

6) Nameless or unnamed: a n o n _ m _ _ _

7) Write the word for this picture and make sure you use a *y* for the /i/ sound.

8 Creating characters

A Visit to Grandpa's

In the middle of the night I woke from a dream full of whips, lariats as long as serpents, and runaway coaches on mountain passes … and I heard the old man in the next room crying, "Gee-up!" and "Whoa!" and trotting his tongue on the roof of his mouth.

It was the first time I had stayed in grandpa's house. The floorboards had creaked like mice as I climbed into bed … It was a mild summer night, but curtains had flapped and branches beaten against the window. I had pulled the sheets over my head, and soon was roaring and riding in a book.

"Whoa there, my beauties!" cried grandpa. His voice sounded very young and loud, and his tongue had powerful hooves, and he made his bedroom into a great meadow. I thought I would see if he was ill, or had set the bedclothes on fire, for my mother had said that he lit his pipe under the blankets, and had warned me to run to his help if I smelt smoke in the night … When I saw there was a light in the room I felt frightened, and as I opened the door I heard grandpa shout, "Gee-up!" as loudly as a bull with a megaphone.

He was sitting straight up in bed and rocking from side to side as though the bed were on a rough road; the knotted edges of the counterpane were his reins; his invisible horses stood in a shadow beyond the bedside candle. Over a white flannel nightshirt he was wearing a red waistcoat with walnut-size brass buttons. The over-filled bowl of his pipe smouldered among his whiskers like a little burning hayrick on a stick. At the sight of me his hands dropped from the reins and lay blue and quiet, the bed stopped still on a level road, he muffled his tongue into silence, and the horses drew softly up.

"Is there anything the matter, grandpa?" I asked, though the clothes were not on fire. His face in the candlelight looked like a ragged quilt pinned upright on the black air and patched all over with goat-beards.

He stared at me mildly. Then he blew down his pipe, scattering the sparks and making a high, wet dog-whistle of the stem, and shouted: "Ask no questions."

After a pause, he said slyly: "Do you ever have nightmares, boy?"

I said: "No."

"Oh, yes, you do," he said.

I said I was woken by a voice that was shouting to horses.

"What did I tell you?" he said. "You eat too much. Who ever heard of horses in a bedroom?"

He fumbled under his pillow, brought out a small, tinkling bag, and carefully untied its strings. He put a sovereign in my hand, and said: "Buy a cake." I thanked him and wished him goodnight.

Dylan Thomas

Speak about it

Is it possible to tell what a person is like by the way that they act?
Would this passage have been so funny if someone else other than a grandfather had been used? Why?

Comprehension

1) Where was the narrator staying?

2) What was the narrator dreaming about?

3) When he woke up, what did he hear? Why was this surprising?

4) Describe the kind of house that he was staying in.

5) The narrator talks about 'roaring and riding in a book'. What kind of book do you think this was? Explain why.

6) How does grandpa explain his strange behaviour?

Language focus

1) Do you think the behaviour of grandpa is strange? Explain why. What is he doing?

2) Use a chart to list evidence from the passage.

What he says ...	
What he does ...	
How he acts ...	
What he looks like ...	

3) From each of these sections draw a conclusion. Write: **I think he is a ... kind of person because ...**

4) Show how grandpa is clever in the way he convinces the narrator of what happened. How does he make sure his grandson will believe him? What does this show about him?

Links to writing

1) Write about how you would expect a grandpa to behave: 'My perfect grandpa'. Would he act in a fun way like the character in this story? Would he be serious? What would he look like? How would he dress?

2) Imagine that you come into school one morning and find your friends behaving in a strange way. How do they explain it so that they don't feel too foolish?

   Use a chart like the one above to plan your detail.

   What will the opening situation be?

   How will you react?

   How will you end your story?

9 Words from other countries

You will know from history that the British Isles have been invaded many times in the past.

Every invader has left some of their language behind. This sometimes makes spelling difficult!

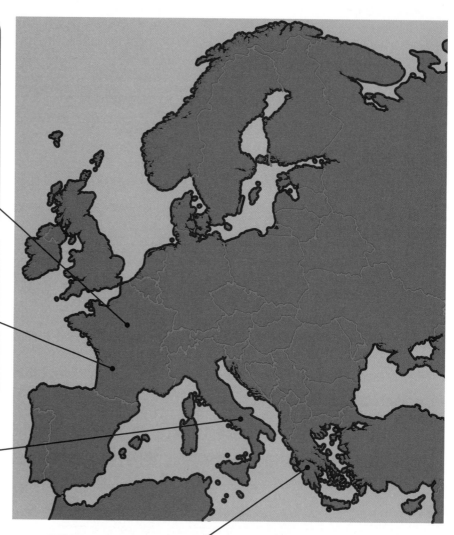

Words like **antique**, **unique** and **league** come from old French words. These end with a suffix where the /**g**/ sound is spelled **-gue** and the /**k**/ sound spelled **-que**. The /**k**/ sound is a 'hard' sound.

Words like **chef**, **chalet** and **chauffeur** come from old French words, where their beginnings (prefixes) with the /**sh**/ sound are spelled **ch-**. Note that this is a 'soft' sound.

Words like **science**, **scene** and **scissors** come from ancient Latin words. The 'soft' /**s**/ sound is spelled **sc-**.

Words like **chorus**, **chemist** and **character** come from ancient Greek words. The hard /**k**/ sound is spelled **ch-**.

Speak about it

Find out when the Romans invaded the British Isles.
Find out when the French invaded the British Isles.
The Greeks never invaded. Who do you think brought the Greek words with them?
Did any other people invade Britain? What languages did they speak?
Do you know of any words that they left behind?

Comprehension

1) What is the name for the beginning of a word that comes from another language?

2) What is the name for the ending of a word that comes from another language?

3) Which sounds are 'hard sounds'? Which country do they come from?

4) Which sounds are 'soft sounds'? Which country do they come from?

5) Look up any of these words from other countries that you do not understand in a dictionary. Write sentences to show you know what they mean.

Language focus

1) Which countries do you think these words come from? Why?

> anchor   chameleon   synagogue   school   tongue   argue
> fascinate   dialogue   Christmas   champagne   brochure   chandelier
> chivalry   plague   disciple   scent   adolescent   muscle

2) Fill in the missing letters in these words. Check your answers in a dictionary. Which country do they come from? How do you know?

   a. va_ _ _   b. _ _emistry

   c. discothe _ _ _   d. a _ _ end

   e. para _ _ ute   f. de _ _ end

   g. _ _ aos   h. mousta _ _ e

   i. ro _ _ _   j. bouti _ _ _

3) Use the correct word in these sentences. Which country do they come from? Check the spelling in a dictionary.

   a. _____ means the only one of its kind.

   b. Muslims pray in a _____.

   c. At an exhibition you can find all the paintings in the printed _____.

   d. You can whip up egg whites stiffly to make _____.

Links to writing

1) Find a dictionary that looks at where words come from – an **etymological** dictionary. Look up the words below from another country. Make your own dictionary using the words here and include others from the same country. Where do all the words below come from?

> pizza   opera   umbrella   piano   spaghetti   studio

10 Similes

In this poem the words give us an impression of how cold affects the world.

From 'The Warm and the Cold'

Freezing dusk is closing

Like a slow trap of steel

On trees and roads and hills and all

That they can no longer feel.

But the carp is in its depth

Like a planet in its heaven.

And the badger in its bedding

Like a loaf in the oven.

And the butterfly in its mummy

Like a viol in its case.

And the owl in its feathers

Like a doll in its lace.

Freezing dusk has tightened

Like a nut screwed tight

On the starry aeroplane

Of the soaring night.

But the trout is in its hole

Like a chuckle in a sleeper.

The hare strays down the highway

Like a root going deeper.

The snail is dry in the outhouse

Like a seed in a sunflower.

The owl is pale on the gatepost

Like a clock on its tower.

Ted Hughes

viol – a kind of violin

chuckle – a bolt

Speak about it

What is a **simile**?
What words does it have to contain?
Find some examples of similes in the poem.
What is being compared?
How is a simile different from a metaphor?
How do similes help you to imagine things?

Comprehension

1) Which words tell us about the speed of the cold coming?

2) Quote the simile that shows that the badger is warm in his burrow.

3) Explain why the butterfly is described as being in 'its mummy'.

4) Where is the snail sleeping to escape the cold?

5) What is it compared to? Does this seem like an effective simile? Why?

6) What can be seen of the owl on its gatepost that reminds the poet of 'a clock on its tower'?

Language focus

1) Identify the similes in the poem. Write the words **like** or **as** in them.

2) Beside each one, write what two things are being compared.

3) Decide what extra information the similes add. You could make a chart to record your findings.

Simile	Two things compared	Information added
Dusk is closing like a slow trap of steel		

4) Explain how the extra information makes you feel about what is being described.

Links to writing

1) Complete the following similes with your own ideas.

   The drink was as cold as ...   **The lorry was as wide as ...**   **The snow fell like ...**

2) Write your own simile poem. Use the following format. Remember that the words have to rhyme. You can be as silly as you like!

   Imagine a coat   **Imagine a ...**

   As wide as a boat   **As ... as ...**

11 Metaphors

Pigeons

They paddle with staccato feet

In powder-pools of sunlight,

Small blue busybodies

Strutting like fat gentlemen

With hands clasped

Under their swallowtail coats;

And, as they stump about,

Their heads like tiny hammers   *Similie*

Tap at imaginary nails

In non-existent walls.

Elusive ghosts of sunshine   M

Slither down the green gloss

Of their necks in an instant, and are gone.

Summer hangs drugged from sky to earth   M

In limpid fathoms of silence: → M

Only warm dark dimples of sound

Slide like slow bubbles   Si~

From the contented throats.

Raise a casual hand – with one quick gust

They fountain into air.

Richard Kell

Speak about it

A simile is **like** something – discuss the pigeons as 'like fat gentlemen', and what else could they be like?

A metaphor **is** something – discuss the pigeons as 'fat gentlemen', and what else could they be?

How do metaphors help you to imagine things?

Find some examples of metaphor from the poem.

Why are they more difficult to spot than similes?

Comprehension

1) What does **staccato** mean? You may have to look in a dictionary.

2) How does this help you to imagine the way a pigeon moves?

3) The author imagines pigeons to be like 'fat gentlemen'. How are these men dressed?

4) How does he imagine the heads of pigeons to move?

5) Which words suggest that a pigeon's feathers are shiny? gloss

6) What impression of summer does the poem give? Does this link with your view?

7) How does the poet describe the pigeons flying away? Is it a good image? Why?

Language focus

1) Identify the metaphors in the poem. Beside each one, write what things are being compared.

2) Decide what extra information the metaphors add. You could make a chart to record your findings.

Metaphor	Things compared	Information added
They paddle with staccato feet		

3) Explain how the extra information helps you to imagine the picture of the pigeons.

4) Decide which of the following are similes and which are metaphors. Explain why.

   a. Her eyes shone like diamonds.   **b.** The truck flew down the empty road.
   c. The sea is a mirror for the clouds. M   **d.** They were as quiet as mice. S

Links to writing

1) If you take a metaphor literally, then it makes an impossible situation, e.g. **It's raining cats and dogs**. Make a list of more metaphors like this.

2) One form of metaphor is to describe something as if it was a human being or animal. This is called personification, e.g. **The sea is a hungry dog, giant and grey …**
Continue with this poem about the sea, writing more metaphors about the sea as if it were an animal. Make a list of what the sea is like and what it does. What animal does it remind you of? How does this animal behave?

12 Creating settings: suspense

A Night on the Moors

The moon was hidden behind the clouds, and in among the trees the night was pitch black. David moved carefully and silently through the undergrowth, feeling the ground in front of him with his hands as he went. He knew he was near the hide-out. Suddenly a twig snapped under his foot. It made a crack like a pistol shot. He stopped. He was shaking with terror. He was certain that the sentries, alert and armed, had heard him. He waited five minutes, hardly daring to breathe. Down below him, he could just see the inky black water of Loch Ness. He wished he had never offered to take the message.

In the distance an owl hooted and a fox barked; then everything went silent again. David started to creep forward, more carefully than ever. It seemed hours before he came to the path which led to the hide-out below the cliff. 'Halt!' a voice called from the darkness.

David stopped. He could just see the outline of the sentry. His first thought was to turn and run. At that moment the moon broke through the clouds and the moonlight glinted on the barrel of the sentry's rifle. Behind the rifle, the face of the sentry peered down at him. Slowly he got to his feet and put his hands above his head.

Speak about it

What do you understand by **suspense**?
Is it necessary in all stories?
How does it make the reader feel?
Which kinds of stories might not need it?
What things do you think are necessary to create suspense? Give examples from books or films.

Comprehension

1) Why was the night pitch black?

2) Which words tell you how David moved? Why should he have to do this?

3) What did he do that made him terrified? Why was this?

4) Quote the words that prove that the hide-out was guarded.

5) Why was David on this dangerous journey?

6) When David was stopped, what was his first thought?

Language focus

1) The author creates suspense because we are afraid and uncertain about the situation of the character. List what we know about the situation of the character. Why is he there? What is he doing? How is he feeling? Why are we afraid for David?

2) The location is also important. Make notes about what we learn of the place, other people there and the time of day (was it light or dark?). Is it scary? Is it dangerous?

3) List the adverbs and adjectives used by the author, e.g. **carefully** and **silently**. Say what information they add to create the suspense.

Links to writing

1) Look carefully at: 'He knew he was near the hide-out. Suddenly a twig snapped under his foot. It made a crack like a pistol shot. He stopped. He was shaking with terror.' Notice:

   ● the use of short sentences.   ● the **sound** words.   ● the use of the simile.

   Rewrite the passage using longer sentences. What difference does it make to the suspense?

2) Imagine that David escapes. Continue with the story as he is on the run. How will you create suspense? Use short sentences when moments get tense – but don't forget longer sentences for description as well.

13 Genre: westerns

From *Shane*

Ledyard was a small, thin-featured man, a peddler or trader who came through every couple of months with things you could not get at the general store in town. He would pack in his stock on a mule-team freighter driven by an old, white-haired Negro who acted like he was afraid even to speak without permission … I did not like him, and not just because he said nice things about me he did not mean for father's benefit. He smiled too much and there was no real friendliness in it.

By the time we were beside the porch, he had swung the horse into our lane and was pulling it to a stop. He jumped down, calling greetings. Father went to meet him. Shane stayed by the porch, leaning against the post.

"It's here," said Ledyard. "The beauty I told you about." He yanked away the canvas covering from the body of the wagon and the sun was bright on a shiny new seven-pronged cultivator lying on its side on the floorboards. "That's the best buy I've toted this haul."

"Hm-m-m-m," said father. "You've hit it right. That's what I've been wanting. But when you start chattering about a best buy that always means big money. What's the tariff?"

"Well, now." Ledyard was slow with his reply. "It cost me more than I figured when we was talking last time. You might think it a bit steep. I don't … You'll make up the difference in no time with the work you'll save with that. Handles so easy even the boy here will be using it before long."

"Pin it down," said father. "I've asked you a question."

Ledyard was quick now. "Tell you what, I'll shave the price … to please a good customer. I'll let you have it for a hundred and ten."

I was startled to hear Shane's voice cutting in quiet and even and plain. "Let you have it? I reckon he will. There was one like that in a store in Cheyenne. List price sixty dollars."

Ledyard shifted part way around … he looked closely at our visitor. The surface smile left his face. His voice held an ugly undertone. "Did anyone ask you to push in on this?"

"No," said Shane, quietly and evenly as before. "I reckon no-one did." He was still leaning against the post. He did not move and he did not say anything more.

Jack Schaeffer

Speak about it

What do you think are the features of a **western**?

Where did you find out about these features?

Can you tell who the **hero** is here? Who is the **villain**? How do you know?

Comprehension

1) What did Ledyard sell?

2) Why did the narrator not like him?

3) What words in the first paragraph tell you that this passage is from a western?

4) When Ledyard arrived, what did Shane do? What might this tell you about him?

5) What was the narrator's father buying? How do they disagree over it?

6) How does Shane intervene? What does this tell us about him?

Language focus

1) Identify features in the passage that would tell you this was from a western. Use a chart to help.

Setting	
Characters	
Events	

2) List any other kinds of details, people or objects that you would expect to find in a western.

3) What do you think happens next? How will it end? Do westerns have a particular way of developing a story? You could continue the story.

Links to writing

1) Design and make a story game about westerns. Make three sets of cards containing pictures for the following aspects:

● setting: Wild West, ranch, town, wagon train, Indian reservation

● characters: hero, villain, Indians, sheriff, mother, child

● events: gunfight in saloon, wagon train attacked, gunfight in street, cattle rustling on ranch

Add some more ideas of your own. Challenge people to take one card from each pile and tell the story. Then write the story based on the card selection.

Remember that the detail you use will be very important to create a picture of the time and place for your reader.

14 Test your grammar, punctuation and spelling

Grammar

Verb inflections and Standard English

Find six errors in the following passage and correct each one.

> It were a dull, grey day but we was as excited as usual for our game.
> There were a good team and we intend to win; if we do, then we
> would've gone up to the next league.

Fronted adverbials

Rewrite each sentence using a fronted adverbial and a comma to emphasise how often or how something is done. These words may help you: *sadly, usually, happily, carefully, angrily, humbly, lazily, quietly*

Example   I go to the cinema.   →   Usually, I go to the cinema.

1) He opened the door.

2) I swim on a Saturday.

3) I stay in bed all day.

4) I ate ice cream.

5) She screamed because she did not get her own way.

6) I cycle to school on the busy road.

Punctuation

Plural *s* or possessive *s*?

Which of these sentences is missing a possessive *s*? Write each word that needs an apostrophe and add the apostrophe in the correct place.

1) The childrens lessons were interrupted.

2) The teachers didn't mind because the boys and girls parents had been notified.

3) Parents permission had been given.

4) The head teacher suggested that the games were viewed in assemblies to minimise disruption.

5) One boys calculator and two girls phones came in handy!

6) The games were amazing.

Beware! Some are plural

Spelling

Spelling common words

Choose and write out the correct spelling for each one.

Example

accident	acksident	acsident

1)	bussiness	business	businness
2)	difficult	dificult	diffickult
3)	urth	eath	earth
4)	knowledge	nowledge	knowlidge
5)	ocasion	occasion	ocassion
6)	separate	separite	sepparate

The sound /u/ spelled as -ou

Fill each gap with a word that has the letters **-ou** for the sound /u/.

Example   You are too *young* to come to the party with me.

1) But I'm your _____ so they'll let me in.

2) The sea is very _____ tonight.

3) We don't want to get into _____.

4) The sign said: 'Do not _____ the animals'.

5) Find one more word that has this spelling of the /u/ sound.

15 Genre: science fiction

From *All Summer in a Day*

'Ready?'

'Ready.'

'Now?'

'Soon.'

'Do the scientists really know? Will it happen today, will it?'

'Look, look; see for yourself!'

The children pressed to each other like so many roses, so many weeds, intermixed, peering out to look for the hidden sun.

It rained.

It had been raining for seven years; thousands upon thousands of days compounded and filled from one end to the other with rain, with the drum and gush of water, with the sweet crystal fall of showers and the concussion of storms so heavy they were tidal waves come over the islands. A thousand forests had been crushed under the rain and grown up a thousand times to be crushed again. And this was the way life was forever on the planet Venus, and this was the schoolroom of the children, of the rocket men and women who had come to a raining world to set up civilisation and live out their lives.

'It's stopping, it's stopping!'

'Yes, yes!'

Margot stood apart from them, from these children who could never remember a time when there wasn't rain and rain and rain. They were all nine years old, and if there had been a day seven years ago, when the sun came out for an hour and showed its face to the stunned world, they could not recall.

Ray Bradbury

Speak about it

What do you think are the features of **science fiction**?
In what kind of places are science fiction stories usually set?
In what time are they usually set?
Where did you find out about these features?
What makes you think that this passage comes from a science fiction book?

English Study Guide: Year 4

Answer Booklet

1 Homophones

Comprehension
1) She whispers so as not to offend him.
2) 'sighing', 'offended'
3) It's in the shape of a mouse's wiggly tail.
4) Because she is looking at the long tail attached to the mouse.
5) She misunderstands the mouse and thinks he's talking about the tail attached to him, rather than the tale he's going to tell.
6) A dog (cur) called Old Fury is teasing a mouse and threatening to kill him because he is bored.
7) *Own answer*

Language focus
1) a. grate – great;
   b. groan – grown;
   c. here – hear;
   d. knot – not;
   e. mail – male;
   f. main – mane
2) a. accept – except;
   b. affect – effect;
   c. ball – bawl;
   d. berry – bury;
   e. brake – break;
   f. fair – fare;
   g. meat – meet;
   h. meddle – medal;
   i. mist – missed;
   j. peace – piece;
   k. plane – plain;
   l. scene – seen
3) *Own answers*
4) a. there – their – they're;
   b. two – too – to;
   c. pair – pear – pare;
   d. heel – heal – he'll;
   e. road – rode;
   f. for – four – fore;
   own answers

Links to writing
1), 2) *Own answers*

2 Sounds and letters

Comprehension
1) eight
2) Pull Santa's sleigh.
3) Holding the reins, guiding the reindeer.
4) He was tired of waiting for the exciting event. He thought it would never happen.
5) No. 'I stopped believing …'

Language focus
1) a. Santa's sleigh is pulled by reindeer.
   b. I heard the horse neigh in the stable.
   c. Half of sixteen is eight.
   d. To take blood, the nurse looked for the vein in his arm.
   e. The lion preys on smaller animals.
   f. Scales are used to check weight.
   g. The freight was loaded onto the barge so it could be taken overseas.
2) grey, prey, they, obey, convey, survey: -ey sound at the end of the word
   pain, stain, remain: -ai sound in the middle of the word
   Own answers

3) sprey, sheikh, vien, obay, surveigh;
   own answers

Links to writing
1), 2) *Own answers*

3 Forms of poetry: ballads

Comprehension
1) The two characters are a mother and son. She refers to him as her son and then refers to his father in the final verse.
2) One brother killing another.
3) He says the blood is his horse's, the hunting dog's and the ox's.
4) She keeps asking where the blood came from. She says the blood is the wrong colour for the horse and points out the hunting dog.
5) He doesn't want to tell where the blood really came from.
6) The blood on his shirt is his brother's. He is probably telling so many lies so that he doesn't get into trouble.
7) Yes, because the boy has murdered another human being, his brother.
8) The story ends with the boy saying he will run away before his father returns. He will find a boat and 'will sail across the sea.'

Language focus
1) Verse 1: The boy says the blood came from the horse.
   Verse 2: The boy says the blood came from his little hunting dog.
   Verse 3: The boy says the blood came from his strong ox.
   Verse 4: The boy confesses it is his brother's blood.
   Verse 5: The boy says he will run away.
2) In each verse the mother asks a question and the boy replies.
3) The beginning is the first verse, the middle is verses 2, 3 and 4 and the last verse is the end of the story.
4) *Own answer*
5) The boy keeps telling lies which the mother doesn't believe.

Links to writing
1), 2), 3), 4) *Own answers*

4 Adding suffixes beginning with vowels

Comprehension
1) Kick the ball nice and high so that it drops towards the far post
2) The goal mouth is 'crowded'.
3) He 'measured his strides back from the ball' and 'took a slow steadying breath.'
4) 'Rich and the keeper collided'
5) 'flailed', 'dived', 'pushed', 'collided' and 'scramble'
6) 'flung' and 'cannoned'

Language focus
1) In single-syllable verbs where a vowel precedes a final consonant, the final consonant doubles when adding a suffix: to slam, slamming, slammed. In words of more than one syllable, it depends on which syllable is stressed – see below.

2) If the stress is on the final syllable, the last letter doubles before adding the suffix: to garden, gardening, garden-ed; to limit, limiting, limited; to begin, beginning, beg-un; to forget, forgetting, forgotten; to prefer, preferring, preferred.
3) If the verb ends in -e and you add -ing, the final -e is dropped as -ei makes a different sound: measure, measuring; described, describing; collided, colliding; scrambled, scrambling; pursued, pursuing; *own answers*.
4) If a verb ends in -y, drop the -y to add -ied: hurried, hurrying; relied, relying; justified, justifying; supplied, supplying; married, marrying.

Links to writing
1) *Own answers*: proves the rule above
2) *Own answers*

5 Investigating non-fiction

Comprehension
1) London covers 1600 km² and has a population of over nine million.
2) The city was founded by the Romans who called it 'Londinium', which is very similar to 'London'.
3) The River Thames runs through the city.
4) The best collection of modern art is at the Tate Modern.
5) You should go to the Natural History Museum.
6) Shakespeare's Globe theatre is on the south bank of the Thames.

Language focus
1) *Not all information from the passage will be expected.*

Facts about London	What to see in London?
capital city	museums
1600 km²	galleries
nine million population	historic buildings
largest city in UK	parks and other forms of entertainment
founded by Romans in AD43	
situated on north bank of river Thames	
tidal	
a port	
mild winters	
some hot summers	
average rainfall of 600 mm	

2) The sub-headings focus on bringing parts of the text to the attention of the reader: basic facts, museums, historic buildings, entertainment venues.
3), 4) *Own answers*

Links to writing
1), 2) *Own answers*

6 Punctuation of direct speech

Comprehension

1) Although he is big, like all giants, he is friendly, not nasty.
2) He is concerned that she is cold; he is concerned about her parents; he is concerned Sophie is missing them.
3) In a cave.
4) An orphanage.
5) That her parents must be missing her.
6) They died.
7) Because she never knew them.

Language focus

1) **a.** 'Is you quite snugly there in your nightie?' he asked. 'You isn't fridgy cold?'
2) **a.** 'Are you ready to go?' she asked.
   b. 'Certainly not,' Ellie replied.
   c. 'But you said to come at four o'clock,' Jamal said.
   d. 'That's not what I said at all,' Mum shouted.
   e. 'How nice to see you. Are you hungry?' I said.
3) **a.** 'Now then,' said the policeman. 'What's going on here?'
   'What a silly question,' replied the workman. 'Can't you see we're digging a hole?'
   b. 'What will you give me for a ride on my new bike?' Tony asked. 'A pound?'
   'A pound? Not likely!' Fred replied.

Links to writing

1), 2) *Own answers*

7 Test your grammar, punctuation and spelling

Grammar

Nouns and pronouns

1) he
2) they
3) his
4) their
5) they
6) we

Replacing pronouns with nouns

1) the people/the children
2) the apple
3) the boys
4) the girls
5) the ball

Punctuation

Inverted commas (speech marks)

We landed in a faraway place beyond the desert.

'It's quite magical,' I gasped.

'Is that all you can say about this mess we have got ourselves into?' Oz replied.

'Well, it is … quite magical. It could be a lot worse!' I replied.

'It could NOT be worse! We are lost like two aliens in the universe!' yelled Oz.

I think he was angry, but I knew I was right and we'd be fine. I just needed time to show him.

Spelling

Adding suffixes beginning with vowels to words of more than one syllable

1) preferring
2) beginning
3) gardening
4) limiting
5) travelling
6) enrolling

The sound /i/ spelled with a y within words

1) myth
2) Egypt
3) gymnastics

---

4) pyramid
5) mystery
6) anonymous
7) bicycle

8 Creating characters

Comprehension

1) He was staying at his grandpa's house.
2) He was dreaming about riding horses.
3) He heard his grandpa shouting "Gee-up!" and "Whoa!". It was surprising because it was the middle of the night.
4) The house is creaky and old.
5) It sounds like an adventure book to do with horses, maybe cowboys and Indians.
6) He tries to make his grandson think he was having a nightmare.

Language focus

1) Grandpa's behaviour seems childish for an old man, and it's a funny thing for anyone to do in the middle of the night.
2), 3) *Own answers*
4) Grandpa is clever because he convinces his grandson that he ate too much and therefore is having nightmares. He gives his grandson money to make sure he believes the explanation. This shows Grandpa is dishonest.

Links to writing

1), 2) *Own answers*

9 Words from other countries

Comprehension

1) prefix
2) suffix
3) ch- sounds like /k/ – Greek
4) ch- sounds like /sh/ – French; sc- sounds like /s/ – Latin
5) *Own answers*

Language focus

1) anchor, chameleon, school, Christmas = Greek
   synagogue, tongue, argue, dialogue, plague, champagne, brochure, chandelier, chivalry = French
   fascinate, disciple, scent, adolescent, muscle = Latin
2) **a.** vague
   b. chemistry
   c. discotheque
   d. ascend
   e. parachute
   f. descend
   g. chaos
   h. moustache
   i. rogue
   j. boutique

   Countries: -gue, -que = France; soft ch- = France; sc- = Latin; hard ch- = Greek

3) **a.** 'Unique' means the only one of its kind = French
   b. Muslims pray in a mosque = French
   c. Some London houses have a wall plaque to show someone important lived there = French
   d. Because I have no cash, I'll pay for the clothes by cheque = French

Links to writing

1) All the words come from Italy.
2) *dent-de-lion* = dandelion; *karwan* = caravan; *klimatos* = climate; *own answers*

10 Similes

Comprehension

1) 'closing' and 'slow'
2) 'And the badger in its bedding/Like a loaf in the oven'.
3) Because it is in a cocoon.

---

4) In the outhouse.
5) 'a seed in a sunflower' and *own answer*
6) The owl's face reminds the poet of the clock's face.

Language focus

1) Example: 'But the carp is in its depth/Like a planet in its heaven.'
2) Example: A fish in water is being compared to a planet in space.
3) Example: It makes the fish seem like it is floating, silent and still.
4) *Own answer*

Links to writing

1), 2) *Own answers*

11 Metaphors

Comprehension

1) **Staccato** means disjointed and separate.
2) It might make you imagine the pigeons moving in a jerky way.
3) He imagines them 'With hands clasped/ Under their swallowtail coats'; old-fashioned coats, short at the front and long and pointed at the back.
4) He imagines their heads like 'tiny hammers' tapping at 'imaginary nails'.
5) 'Elusive', 'slither' and 'green gloss'
6) Summer seems slow, hot and silent. *Own answer*
7) The pigeons 'fountain into air', which makes them seem like a sudden rush of water shooting up.

Language focus

1) **a.** 'small blue busybodies' compares pigeons with people who get involved with other people's business.
   b. 'elusive ghosts of sunshine' compares the sun with ghosts.
   c. 'summer hangs drugged' compares the summer with someone sleepy with medicine.
   d. 'limpid fathoms of silence' compares silence with being deep underwater.
   e. 'warm dark dimples of sound' compares sound with being deep underwater.
   f. 'they fountain into air' compares the flying flock to a fountain of water.
2) **a.** It seems as if the pigeons move quickly, whispering and gossiping with each other.
   b. It seems as if the sun shines briefly on the birds' feathers; that you look and it is gone.
   c. It makes the summer seem sleepy and slow.
   d. It makes the silence seem heavy and deep.
   e. It seems like sound comes in little pockets; that the sounds are soft and comforting.
   f. It seems like the pigeons fly up suddenly and break the hot summer's day like a cool refreshing fountain.
3) The metaphors help you paint pictures in your head of what the birds are like.
4) **a.** simile – compares eyes to diamonds using 'like'
   b. metaphor – compares a truck to something that flies without using 'as' or 'like'
   c. metaphor – compares the sea to a mirror without using 'as' or 'like'
   d. simile – compares people to mice using 'like'

Links to writing

1), 2) *Own answers*

12 Creating settings: suspense

Comprehension

1) The moon was hidden behind the clouds, which turned the night pitch black.
2) The words 'carefully' and 'silently' tell us how David moved. He was trying not to be noticed.
3) He snapped a twig as he moved, which made a very loud noise. This terrified him because he didn't want to get caught.
4) There are several references in the text to what the 'sentries' said and did.
5) David was carrying a message.
6) His first thought was to run away.

Language focus

1) David is there because he is delivering a message; he is creeping as quietly as possible through the undergrowth; he is 'shaking with terror' and 'hardly daring to breathe'; we are not sure if he will be caught or not, and we do not know what will happen to him if he is caught.
2) He is near Loch Ness, deep in the undergrowth; there are sentries nearby, but he does not know where; it is night time and it is dark; there are scary noises; we know it is dangerous because of the way David is behaving and because of the actions of the sentries.
3) **Adverbs:** 'carefully', 'silently', 'suddenly', 'hardly', 'slowly'
   Adjectives: 'pitch-black', 'alert', 'armed', 'inky', 'black', 'glinted'
   Slow and quiet adverbs keep us in suspense. The suspense is then broken dramatically by a quick adverb like 'suddenly'. The adjectives add to the suspense by making everything seem dark and dangerous.

Links to writing

1), 2) *Own answers*

13 Genre: westerns

Comprehension

1) He sold things you could not get at the general store in town.
2) Ledyard says kind but insincere things about the narrator to please the narrator's father, and he smiles a lot but not in a genuine way.
3) 'mule-team'
4) Shane did not go to meet Ledyard but stayed by the house; this might tell us that Shane does not like Ledyard.
5) A cultivator – a piece of farm machinery; Ledyard and the narrator's father disagree about the price of the cultivator.
6) Shane says that he saw a cultivator fifty dollars cheaper in a store. He clearly thinks Ledyard is trying to cheat the narrator's father.

Language focus

1) **Setting:** they live out of town; a general store is mentioned; the house has a porch; they live down a lane; they are buying farm machinery so it must be in the countryside
   Characters: a cunning peddler; a white-haired negro working for the peddler; a farmer; a farmer's son (the narrator); a mysterious, suspicious character (Shane)
   Events: trading goods; people travelling by horse and cart; characters scared or intimidated by others; characters trying to trick other characters out of money; conflict and disagreement between characters
2) Some examples: cowboys, Indians, deserts, cacti, sunsets, horses, gunfights, ambushes, gold, pretty girls, villains, heroes, saloon bars

3) *Own answer*

Links to writing

1) *Own answer*

14 Test your grammar, punctuation and spelling

Grammar

Verb inflections and Standard English

It **was** a dull, grey day but we **were** as excited as usual for our game.

There **was** a good team and we **intended** to win; if we **did**, then we **would go** up to the next league.

Fronted adverbials

1) Quietly, he opened the door.
2) Usually, I swim on a Saturday.
3) Lazily, I stay in bed all day.
4) Happily, I ate ice cream.
5) Angrily, she screamed because she did not get her own way.
6) Carefully, I cycle to school on the busy road.

Punctuation

Plural s or possessive s?

1) children's
2) boys' and girls'
3) parents'
4) Plural
5) boy's/ girls'
6) Plural

Spelling

Spelling common words

1) business
2) difficult
3) earth
4) knowledge
5) occasion
6) separate

The sound /u/ spelled as -ou

1) cousin
2) rough
3) trouble
4) touch
5) Accept all correct and reasonable answers.

15 Genre: science fiction

Comprehension

1) The story is set on the planet Venus.
2) They had come to 'set up civilisation and live out their lives.'
3) The children were looking for the sun.
4) This might seem surprising to us because we see the sun all the time.
5) 'It had been raining for seven years'. *Own answer*
6) The events described are so unusual that they might make you curious about the story.
7) It seems that unlike all the other children, she can remember a time when it wasn't raining.

Language focus

1) 'It had been raining for seven years', 'this was the way life was forever on the planet Venus', 'rocket men and women', 'a raining world'
2) **Setting:** a schoolroom on the planet Venus; islands; forests
   Characters: scientists; rocket men and women; children who can't remember the sun; Margot
   Events: people who rely on scientists for information; people excited to see the sun for the first time; constant rain for seven years; heavy storms; people who came to set up a civilisation
3) Some examples: strange planets; journeys through space; time travel; strange

creatures and civilisations; evil characters; good characters; powerful characters; weak characters; war; spaceships
4) *Own answer*

Links to writing

1), 2) *Own answers*

16 Presenting poetry

Comprehension

1) It is high above him, as if it is touching the sky.
2) a ball
3) tiny insects
4) whistling and whispering
5) He is holding it tight and the wind is making it strain.
6) It is evening and getting dark.

Language focus

1), 2), 3), 4) *Own answers*
5) '... like a ball ... ': the earth from up high is round like a ball; '... as creeping bees ...': animals such as oxen seen from high up look like small insects creeping. *Own answer*

Links to writing

1), 2) *Own answers*

17 Suffixes – the 'shun' sound

Comprehension

1) -tion
2) 'fashion' and 'cushion'
3) Words ending in -de make a big change.
4) **a.** to talk about in a general way = discussion
   b. to do things again and again = repetition
   c. a person involved in governing the country = politician

Language focus

1) If the word ends in an -e, drop the final -e: celebration, inflation, separation, protection, invention. *Own answer*
2) If the word ends in a -t, change this to -ss before adding -ion: possession, confession, impression, submission, omission. *Own answer*
3) If the word ends in -de, drop the -de before adding -sion. If the word ends in -se, drop the final -e in before adding -ion: television, confusion, erosion, exclusion, explosion. *Own answer*

Links to writing

1), 2) *Own answers*

18 Explanations

Comprehension

1) Email is quick and it allows you to send the same message to a group of people at the same time.
2) So that people can decide whether or not your message is relevant to them.
3) The length of your email might depend on why you are writing; an informal, chatty email will be much longer than a formal email passing on important information.
4) If, for example, you are writing to a relative in Australia, your style will be more informal than if you were writing to an important person asking them to visit your school.
5) We are being warned that emails can be forwarded and copied to other people very easily, so it is important not to be rude about anyone.

Language focus

1) Computing books, the Internet, user manuals, information leaflets, people who use email.
2) **Title that states what it's about:** 'How do I get started with an email?'
   Explains one thing at a time: 'Step 1', 'Step 2', etc.

b. We have a box that was made two hundred years ago for storing cheese.

2) *Own answers*

25 Commas to mark clauses

Comprehension

1) It was spring when Grendel attacked.

2) Grendel was known as *'the Night-Stalker'* and *'the Death-Shadow'*.

3) *'Snarling in rage'* are the words that tell you he is angry.

4) Beowulf first saw Grendel's shadow and then his green eyes.

5) Grendel does not care about killing men because as he reached out to kill his first victim he was *'laughing in his throat'*.

Language focus

1) *Own answers*

2) **a.** When I heard the scream, I phoned the police.

b. If she is nervous, she must tell her mum.

c. Although I am afraid of flying, I travelled by plane.

d. Since their office burned down, they do not reply to letters.

e. After I have been to the festival, I will revise for my exams.

3) *Own answers*

Links to writing

1), 2) *Own answers*

26 Time and cause

Comprehension

1) The Tripod was *'some miles away'*.

2) The only place to hide were the bushes on the hillside.

3) They *'flung'* themselves in, *'burrowed'* themselves down and *'crouched'* in the bushes.

4) Henry could tell they were really large because the ground began to shake more and more as they approached.

5) *'plunged across the blue'* and *'black against the arc of the sky,'* tell us that Henry is looking upwards.

6) The whistling sound was the sound of bushes being ripped out of the ground and tossed through the air; the Tripod was trying to expose Henry and Beanpole.

Language focus

1) *'fast'* describes how the Tripods were coming; *'fast'* later describes the whipping sound of the bushes being uprooted; *'fearfully'* describes the way Henry glanced; *'plainly'* describes how Henry and Beanpole will be seen by the Tripods. If you took the adverbs away you would not know how quickly the Tripods were advancing or how Henry felt.

2) *Own answer*

3) If you take *'fearfully'* out of the sentence then you do not learn how Henry is reacting to the situation.

Links to writing

1), 2) *Own answers*

27 Apostrophes for possession

Comprehension

1) Liverpool beat Sunderland.

2) The organisers apologised publicly, which showed their embarrassment.

3) Webb couldn't collect his medal because he had changed shirts with an opponent and was refused entry to the directors' box.

4) He was given his medal in the dressing room afterwards.

5) **Fictitious** means 'made up'. He made up a report for a match that never took place.

6) Both clubs were fined for their part in the deception.

Language focus

1) *'winners' medals'*, *'the other team's medals'*, *'the organisers' embarrassment'*, *'the directors' box'*, *'Webb's loss'*, *'Devon's Amateur Football Association'*, *'Woodland Fort's 2–0 'victory''*, *'Combination League's final match'*, *'the manager's response'*

2) *winners' medals* (the medals belonging to the winners)

the other team's medals (the medals belonging to the other team)

the organisers' embarrassment (the embarrassment of the organisers)

the directors' box (the box of the directors)

Webb's loss (the loss of Webb)

Devon's Amateur Football Association (the Amateur Football Association of Devon)

Woodland Fort's 2–0 'victory' (the 2–0 victory of Woodland Fort)

Combination League's final match (the final match of the Combination League)

the manager's response (the response of the manager)

3) **a.** This should not be a possessive apostrophe, simply a plural -es ending

b. **Children** is the plural of **child** so the apostrophe should go before the -s, not after it.

c. The author's name is Dickens (not Dicken), therefore apostrophe -s (Dickens's) or simply an apostrophe should be added after the -s (Dickens')

d. There are two cats therefore the apostrophe should go after the -s of 'cats'.

Links to writing

1), 2) *Own answers*

28 Test your grammar, punctuation and spelling

Grammar

Personal pronouns, possessive pronouns and adverbials

(personal) pronoun: she, them, they

possessive pronoun: ours, mine, theirs

adverbial: swiftly, quite, happily, in addition

Verb inflections

Verb	Present	Past	Present perfect	Present continuous
to have	he has	he had	he has had	he is having
to buy	she buys	she bought	she has bought	she is buying
to fall	we fall	we fell	we have fallen	we are falling
to travel	they travel	they travelled	they have travelled	they are travelling
to do	you do	you did	you have done	you are doing

Punctuation

Commas with fronted adverbials

1) In the first instance, we must go to collect the car.

2) After we've checked in, we can explore the place.

3) In the middle of the night, they crept out.

4) Creeping silently and steadily, they breathed in the night air.

5) Jumping into the sea, they laughed and splashed.

6) Before night fell, they were back home safe and sound.

Spelling

Common words

1) surprise

2) favourite

3) experience

4) paragraph

5) library

6) opposite

The suffix /shun/

1) invention

2) musician

3) possession

4) expression

5) magician

6) injection

7) extension

8) admission

Describes how and why things work: '*This is because people receiving your message …*'

Describes what can happen if: '*Your email can easily be forwarded to hundreds of others – so don't be rude about anyone!*'

Uses mostly present tense: '*An email message has …*', '*The message text is …*'

Uses features to make reading easier: a clear title, an introduction that defines the subject, paragraphs that explain how or why in the correct order, a final paragraph to sum up or give important extra information

Uses connectives of time: Next, then
Uses connectives to say why things happen: Because

Links to writing
1) option, junction, question, expression
2), 3) *Own answers*

19 Advertisments
Comprehension
1) It makes the product sound important and more effective.
2) Important words can be capitalised to make them stand out.
3) Vets are specialists, and a specialist's opinion can be persuasive. In this text the vets think that '*this will make cats healthier and live longer*'.
4) *Own answer*
5) It might be a private advertisement taken from a newspaper where it costs to advertise per word.
6) '*in.*' is an abbreviation for 'inches' and '*ono*' is an abbreviation for 'or nearest offer'.

Language focus
1) '*new*', '*extra*', '*healthy*', '*special*'
2) a.–j. *Own answers*
These words cannot be made into comparatives or superlatives by adding -*er* or -*est* suffixes, you must use 'more' or 'the most'

Links to writing
1), 2) *Own answers*

20 Reading and interpreting playscripts
Comprehension
1) She is treated like a slave because her father, Baron Hardup, married the '*dreadful*' Sinistra.
2) Buttons takes a special interest in Cinderella because he likes her a lot.
3) We know Sinistra is unpleasant because she is rude to Buttons and she tells the audience to shut up.
4) The audience respond by booing her.
5) Stage directions are important so that the characters know how to speak a line, how to behave, and where to move.
6) '*What chores?*' sounds like 'what's yours', which is an invitation to get somebody a drink.

Language focus
1) Answers will be varied, i.e. need a kitchen, animals, vat of custard.
2) a. '*Scene: the kitchen …*' etc.
   b. '*quietly*', '*shouting*', '*screaming from the wings*', '*growls*', '*waking up*', etc.
   c. '*steps to the front of the stage*', '*bashful*' '*to the front of the stage*', '*she hits him around the head*', etc.
3) *Own answers*
4) Baron Hardup – as in 'hard up for money' and Sinistra as in 'sinister'

Links to writing
1), 2) *Own answers*

21 Test your grammar, punctuation and spelling
Grammar
Nouns and pronouns to avoid confusion across sentences
Hyenas look like dogs and are sometimes thought to laugh because of the strange noise **they** make. Spotted hyenas live in southern Africa and striped **hyenas** live further north. **Hyenas** are scavengers, which means that **they** eat food that has been killed by other animals. **They** feed at night and their teeth and jaws are very strong. In the daytime, **hyenas** sleep in holes or caves.

Apostrophes for plurals and possession
1) boys
2) girls
3) boys'
4) girl's
5) boys
6) boys

Punctuation
Commas before fronted adverbials
1) In a few minutes, I will get up.
2) Very quietly, she tiptoed across the floor.
3) At first, they felt a bit shy.
4) In the end, we all made friends.
5) Despite the slightly wobbly start, it was a good day.
6) Silently, I slipped out of the room.

Spelling
The suffix -ation
1) adoration
2) information
3) preparation
4) separation
5) dictation
6) relaxation

Commonly misspelled words
It's **always** good to keep busy. So if you are **travelling** a long way, take some things to do so you are not **disappointed** or bored. If **you're** going on holiday, take lots of **activities**. If you **enjoy** sport, then pack any **equipment** you may need. If you like to read, then **ensure** you have books or an e-book reader or **tablet**. And remember, boredom **disappears** in a flash when you are busy.

22 Organising ideas around a theme
Comprehension
1) Kaliya had five heads and was large enough to crush a human.
2) He lived '*under the darkest whirlpools of the Yamuna River*'.
3) Kill people and animals, and destroy buildings and crops.
4) Krishna was nearly twelve years old and he was a cowherd.
5) He was '*floating along casually, mockingly*'.
6) Krishna took a head under each arm and danced heavily with his feet on the other three heads.

Language focus
1) '*Krishna was almost twelve years old …*'
   – A change of person
   '*One day a group of cowherds …*'
   – A change of time
   '*Krishna collected a group of brave friends …*' – A change of topic
   '*Having done their dirty deed …*'
   – A change of person
   '*Krishna took one flying leap …*'
   – A change of person
   '*Kaliya felt …*' – A change of person
   '*He decided to dive into his underwater court.*' – A change of place
   '*Krishna held his breath …*' – A change of person

'*Having killed two of Kaliya's heads …*'
– A change of topic
2) Topic sentence: '*Those were the days of boiling hot summers.*' Points to illustrate it: the road, the blinds, the ground, the silence.

Links to writing
1) A storm at night – you need shelter – old caravan – you knock – you shout – nothing happens – so…what's in there? – you go in.
2) *Own answer*

23 Standard English
Comprehension
1) The language is appropriate for the audience.
2) When speaking to a teacher, for example.
3) '*He ran real quick.*'
4) '*I've just ate my tea.*'
5) '*I didn't say nothing.*'
6) '*The book what I bought.*'

Language focus
1) He ran really quickly. They were after him because he was reading one of those books.

   I've just eaten my tea, but we were out when it happened.

   I didn't say anything to anyone. The book that I bought was different.

   I never do anything on Fridays, so the place was dead quiet.

   I really like it when Joshua comes around.
2) a. I didn't see any snakes.
   b. We painted the picture beautifully.
   c. There were two clocks in the market square.
   d. My uncle gave me a new computer for my birthday.
   e. George did his homework at the weekend.
   f. The two dogs were fighting in the street.
3) a. 'I haven't done anything!' shouted the man.
   b. He ran away really quickly.
   c. We did the washing-up after lunch.
   d. Those two girls weren't allowed out to the cinema.
   e. 'He doesn't know anything. I already asked him.'
   f. Look in that cupboard that's to your left.
   g. I don't want any trouble from you.

Links to writing
1), 2) *Own answers*

24 Pronouns
Comprehension
1) nouns
2) They stop the repetition of the same nouns.
3) It would be very boring and monotonous.
4) **he** or **she** replaces a male or female person (or animal).
5) Pronouns such as **them** and **they**.

Language focus
1) a. Ranjit is very late. He has been playing with friends.
   b. Ranjit was playing with his dog and he was filthy.
   c. Ranjit's dog was huge. It was called Rover.
   d. Ranjit phoned his mum and asked her if tea was ready.
   e. Ranjit's mum called him back. She was worried.
2) a. We met the old lady in the supermarket.
   b. He was more tired than we were.
   c. The teacher liked him more than her.
   d. We listened carefully to them.

Links to writing
1) a. We met an old man whose beard was long and grey and a little boy.

Comprehension

1) Where is this story set?

2) Why had all the people gone there in the first place?

3) What were the children all looking for?

4) Why does this seem surprising to us?

5) How long had it been raining? Do you find this surprising? Why?

6) How does this kind of information make you feel about the story?

7) Why was Margot different from the rest of the children?

Language focus

1) What phrases in the passage tell you immediately that this story is not set in our own time or in our own world?

2) Identify the other features in the passage that would tell you this was from a science fiction story. Use a chart to help:

Setting	
Characters	
Events	

3) List any other kinds of details, people or objects that you would expect to find in a science fiction story. Where have you found out about these things?

4) What do you think happens next? How will it end? Do science fiction stories have a particular way of developing? You could continue the story.

Links to writing

1) Continue with this science fiction story. Why has it been raining for so long on Venus? What happened to the sun? What happens to Margot?

2) Create some lists of settings, characters and events that you could choose from to write a science fiction story, for example:

● setting: in the future, another planet, spaceship, alien world, space

● characters: hero, villain, captain of spaceship, aliens, boy, girl, robot

● events: finding new planet, aliens fighting back, bad things happening to the world, spaceship breaks down, time travel

16 Presenting poetry

High

Fly, kite!

High!

Till you touch the sky!

Stoop, whistling in the wind;

And whisper down the quivering string.

If, as you soar, you find

The world we tread is like a ball –

With mounds for hills and ponds for seas,

Its oxen small as creeping bees,

Mere bushes its huge trees!

But, ah, the dew begins to fall,

The evening star to shine,

Down you must sink to earth again – an earth, I mean, like mine.

Walter de la Mare

Speak about it

In what sort of weather is it best to fly a kite?

Look up the word 'stoop' in a dictionary. Why would a kite do this?

What other words do you find difficult in this poem? Look them up in a dictionary.

From a kite's point of view, is everything on earth big or small? Why?

Which lines in the poem rhyme? Can you work out the pattern?

Comprehension

1) Explain what the poet sees when he looks up at the kite.

2) What does he imagine the world to look like from the kite's point of view?

3) What would animals look like from the kite's point of view?

4) What noises does the poet hear when he is flying the kite?

5) Why is the string of the kite 'quivering'?

6) Why does he have to stop flying the kite?

Language focus

1) Read the first three lines in different ways for a performance. What difference do these make? The poet uses exclamation marks. How should you say the lines?

   > Fly, kite! *(Try each word loud or soft.)*
   > High! *(Stretch this word out for as long as possible or make it short.)*
   > Till you touch the sky! *(Stress different words – touch … sky …)*

2) Now try the same things with other lines in the poem until you are happy to perform it. Are there any actions you can do while performing the poem?

3) The poem uses 'sound words' (onomatopoeia) to create an atmosphere.

   What sound effects are you creating when you say these words? How can you make them sound better in performance e.g.: **whistling**, **whisper**?

4) Words like **quivering** and **soar** are strong, active verbs. How do they give you a feeling of movement?

5) The poet also uses similes: '… **like a ball** … ', ' … **as creeping bees** … '. What things is he comparing to a ball and to bees? Explain if you think these comparisons are good ones or not.

Links to writing

1) Describe what it feels like to fly a kite on a windy day. Look at the verbs that describe action in the poem. Use some of these.

2) Write an 'I like … ' poem containing sound words. Perform it. Follow the pattern of this one. It does not have to rhyme.

   > *I like music*
   > *The **throb** of the bass*
   > *The **twang** of the guitar*

17 Suffixes – the 'shun' sound

Where you hear a 'shun' sound, never write **sh** except in words like **fashion** and **cushion**.

Most words making this sound end in **-tion**.

But there are other endings. Let's investigate.

-ssion

permit – permi**ss**ion

admit – admi**ss**ion

express – expre**ss**ion

discuss – discu**ss**ion

-tion

invite – invita**tion**

operate – opera**tion**

educate – educa**tion**

add – addi**tion**

act – ac**tion**

attract – attrac**tion**

repeat – repeti**tion**

-sion

revise – revi**sion**

divide – divi**sion**

decide – deci**sion**

include – inclu**sion**

-cian

music – musi**cian**

politics – politi**cian**

What about?

o**cean**

Mar**tian**

Speak about it

What is a suffix?

What suffixes can you see in the words on this page?

Why is the 'shun' sound in spelling such a problem?

Does the 'shun' sound really always sound the same? How are the sounds different in the words on this page?

Are there any words that you do not understand? Use a dictionary to find their meanings.

Comprehension

1) Which is the most popular suffix to make the 'shun' sound?

2) Write two words that really use the letters **sh** to make the 'shun' sound.

3) Which group of words on the page see the biggest change to spelling when the suffix is added?

4) Which words in the lists opposite mean these phrases?

    a. to talk about in a general way

    b. to do things again and again

    c. a person involved in governing the country

Language focus

1) Add **-tion** to these words. Check the spelling in a dictionary. Can you find a rule to help you know when to use **-tion**? Add one word of your own.

    celebrate   inflate   separate   protect   invent

2) Add **-ssion** to these words. Check the spelling in a dictionary. Can you find a rule to help you know when to use **-ssion**? Add one word of your own.

    possess   confess   impress   submit   omit

3) Add **-sion** to these words. Check the spelling in a dictionary. Can you find a rule to help you know when to use **-sion**? Add one word of your own.

    televise   confuse   erode   exclude   explode

Links to writing

1) Which of these words have the wrong suffix? Write the words correctly. Check the spelling in a dictionary.

    fraction   optsion   motion   juncshun   quession

    selection   formation   expretion

2) Write some rules about spelling the 'shun' sound for the rest of your class.

    How many different kinds of spelling are there?

    Which word endings help to form rules?

    Does adding the right suffix change the spelling of the words?

18 Explanations

How do I get started with email?

Email enables anyone with an email address to communicate with any other email address. You can even send the same message to a group of people at the same time.

Creating an email

Step 1 An email message box has two sections: a space for the message header or subject of the email and a space for the person or people who will receive the message. In an email, the subject line should always be completed. This is because people receiving your message may decide not to read the message – or even delete it – if the subject does not seem relevant to them.

Step 2 Next, you will have to write in or insert the email address of the person who you are sending the message to, so that the message goes to the right person.

Step 3 The message text is written in the large space below. You can write as much as you like in this box, but think: is it really necessary? What is the purpose of your email?

Step 4 The language used is important. If you are writing something to a long-lost relative in Australia, you might be writing a great deal in informal language. If you are trying to arrange for an important person to visit your school, then the style and the length will need to be very different.

Step 5 Make sure that the spellchecker is used – emails are famous for being misspelled!

Remember Your email can easily be forwarded to hundreds of others – so don't be rude about anyone! There is no such thing as a secret email. You can't get it back once it's sent.

Speak about it

What is an explanation?
Give some examples of situations when you would have to explain things.
How do you know when an explanation of something is not very good?
How is the setting out of explanations sometimes different from other kinds of text?

Comprehension

1) Can you think of two ways in which email is better than other forms of communication?

2) Why is it important to complete your subject line?

3) How will the purpose of your email decide how much you write?

4) Show how the audience of your email will decide the kind of language you use in it.

5) What do you think the author is warning you about in the sentence 'There is no such thing as a secret email'?

Language focus

1) The author has gathered a lot of information. What kinds of sources could have provided this kind of information?

2) Decide what's needed in an explanation. Identify the features in the passage. Write these in a chart.

	Feature In the passage I found …
Title that states what it's about	
Explains one thing at a time	
Describes how and why things work	
Describes what can happen if …	
Uses mostly present tense	
Uses features to make reading easier	
Uses connectives of time	Next,
Uses connectives to say why something happens	Because

Links to writing

1) Imagine that you have to make a postcard to put beside each computer in class containing this important information. Summarise the material even more. What are the key facts in each section? Which features will you use to make them easily understood? Will you have to write in complete sentences?

2) Rewrite the section about the advantages of email. Start: 'There are many advantages to using email. In the first place …' Decide which one is the better explanation for someone new to email. Say why.

19 Advertisements

Slogan to describe the product – use alliteration

Snuffilacious cats will come sniffing around when you feed them new

SNUFFLE

NEW!

Stress on NEW and different

Just the **BEST** **MOST** economical **MEATIEST** **HEALTHIEST** **CHUNKIEST** cat food on the market!

Superlative adjectives to describe the product

What a treat!

With extra lipids for healthy skin; extra vitamins for healthy eyes; extra calcium for healthy teeth!

Scientific words to help the product to sound better

The College of Veterinarians says that this will make cats healthier and live longer.

Special offer

Buy six packs and get one free!

Words to make your customer feel special

Don't miss out ... do you care enough about your special friend to be a SNUFFLE owner ...?

SNUFFLE on down to your local shop ...

SNUFFLE ... *making a difference to cat health and life-long pleasure!*

For sale: boy's Raleigh bicycle; 21 in. wheel; mountain bike style; sprung saddle; good brakes; excellent condition. £50 o.n.o.

Speak about it

Why do people advertise things?
Where have you seen advertisements?
Are they all the same kind?
How do they try to persuade you to buy things?
Do advertisements always tell the truth?
What are some of the differences between the two kinds of advertisement here? Think about their purpose and their audience.

Comprehension

1) Why do so many advertisements use scientific words to describe their products? E.g. 'extra calcium …'

2) Why do you think so many advertisements use capital letters to spell words out to you?

3) Why do you think the advert mentions vets from the College of Veterinarians? What do they think?

4) Which of all the features mentioned on the opposite page makes the best impression on you?

5) Why is the second advertisement written in a shortened form?

6) What do abbreviations such as **in**. and **o.n.o.** mean?

Language focus

1) Find examples in the advertisement of adjectives being used to persuade you.

2) Advertisements convince you through comparing adjectives, e.g. **This bag is strong. This bag is stronger. This bag is the strongest.** Write sentences that you might see in advertisements using these words.

a. beautiful	**b.** dangerous	**c.** handsome	**d.** pleasant	**e.** delicious
f. good	**g.** far	**h.** little	**i.** many	**j.** bad

What do you notice?

Links to writing

1) Which words would you use to advertise a car for sale? Explain why.

clean   immaculate   spotless   neat

Write the words in sentences in the style of adverts to show that you know the differences in meaning between them.

2) Carry out a class survey into TV advertising. Find out how many use ideas and features from this unit. Also identify features such as: **a happy family life, success in your career, good looks, wealth, popularity, belonging to a special group**.

20 Reading and interpreting playscripts

Pantomime is a traditional form of theatre. It aims to make you laugh. Here is a scene from a pantomime of Cinderella.

Scene: the kitchen. Cinderella in rags asleep. Her two mice cuddled up with her.

BUTTONS (*steps to the front of the stage and looks out to the audience*) Hello, everyone out there.

AUDIENCE Hello … (*quietly*)

BUTTONS (*puts his hand to his ear*) I can't hear you. You can do better than that.

AUDIENCE Hello!! (*shouting*)

BUTTONS That's better. Is everyone happy this afternoon … Well, we'll soon put a stop to that! So here we are in the house of stupid Baron Hardup. He married the dreadful Sinistra and now Cinderella has been put to work in the kitchen as a slave – and he doesn't even notice! And I like her … (*bashful*) … a lot! (*screaming from the wings*) Oh no … here comes the dreadful Sinistra … (*Dame enters*)

DAME What are you doing here, you snivelling little rat …

AUDIENCE Oooooooo

DAME (*to the front of the stage*) And you can all shut up … (*growls*)

AUDIENCE Booo!

BUTTONS I'm doing my chores, madam.

DAME What chores? (*sounds like 'what's yours'*)

BUTTONS Oh, thanks – mine's a cup of coffee and a chocolate biscuit! (*she hits him around the head and chases him around the stage*)

CINDERELLA (*waking up*) Oh no … that wicked stepmother is bothering Buttons again. (*mice trip up stepmother – she falls into a vat of custard*)

Speak about it

What is the story of Cinderella?

How do you know this is a playscript from its layout?

How might the pantomime change the story to make it amusing?

Comprehension

1) Why is Cinderella treated like a slave?

2) Why does Buttons take a special interest in Cinderella?

3) How does the author give us an impression of Sinistra as an unpleasant person?

4) How can you tell that the audience don't like her?

5) Why are the stage directions so important in playscripts?

6) Explain how the joke **What chores?** works.

 Language focus

1) To put on a play you may need 'props'. What would you need on stage for this scene?

2) Find the words:
   a. with which the author introduces the scene
   b. that help actors to know how to speak their lines
   c. that tell the actors how to behave

3) Perform some of the lines without the stage directions. What difference does it make to your performance?

4) One of the jokes here is about the names of the characters. Explain the humour behind **Baron Hardup** and **Sinistra**.

 Links to writing

1) Carry out some research into the history of pantomimes.

   What are the most popular stories?   **What kinds of humour are most popular?**

   What special characters appear in them?   **Where did pantomime originate?**

2) Write the script for another pantomime story, e.g. **Aladdin and the Magic Lamp**. Find out about the story.

   Think about the various ways that you can use language to create humour, e.g. **funny names**, **jokes** and **puns**.

   What other ways will you make people laugh?

21 Test your grammar, punctuation and spelling

Grammar

Nouns and pronouns to avoid confusion across sentences

Choose the right nouns and pronouns to avoid repetition and confusion across sentences.
Rewrite the paragraph, replacing or rewriting each underlined word.

> Hyenas look like dogs and are sometimes thought to laugh because of the strange noise <u>hyenas</u> make. Spotted hyenas live in southern Africa and striped <u>ones</u> live further north. <u>They</u> are scavengers, which means that <u>hyenas</u> eat food that has been killed by other animals. <u>Hyenas</u> feed at night and their teeth and jaws are very strong. In the daytime, <u>they</u> sleep in holes or caves.

Apostrophes for plurals and possession

Choose the correct word and write it.

1) The **(boys/boys')** played on their phones.

2) The **(girls/girl's)** listened to music while sharing headphones.

3) The **(boys'/boy's)** phones bleeped and buzzed.

4) One **(girls/girl's)** headphones broke so she was a bit upset.

5) Two **(boy's/boys)** looked at it for her and fixed it.

6) She thanked the **(boy's /boys)** and bought them a juice.

Punctuation

Commas before fronted adverbials

Rewrite each sentence using a fronted adverbial to emphasise the main point.

Example I went to the cinema last night. → Last night, I went to the cinema.

1) I will get up in a few minutes.

2) She tiptoed across the floor very quietly.

3) They felt a bit shy at first.

4) We all made friends in the end.

5) It was a good day despite the slightly wobbly start.

6) I slipped out of the room silently.

Spelling

The suffix -ation

Write each word with the suffix **-ation** and make spelling adjustments to the new word if necessary.

Example sense → sensation

1) adore

2) inform

3) prepare

4) separate

5) dictate

6) relax

Commonly misspelled words

Read the passage. Find the ten misspellings and write the words correctly.

It's allways good to keep busy. So if you are traveling a long way, take some things to do so you are not disapointed or bored. If your going on holiday, take lots of activites. If you injoy sport, then pack any eqipment you may need. If you like to read, then insure you have books or an e-book reader or tablit. And remember, boredom dissapears in a flash when you are busy.

22 Organising ideas around a theme

From 'The Serpent King'

A myth from India: The Serpent King

Kaliya, the Serpent King, was no ordinary snake. He had five heads and was so large that he could crush humans to death in a matter of seconds. The Serpent King lived under the darkest whirlpools of the Yamuna River and this is where he held his court. Whenever he so wished, he would rise out of the water and lay waste the countryside, ferociously breathing fire and black smoke wherever he went.

Krishna was almost twelve years old by now. Even at this tender age he was the acknowledged leader among his friends and looked upon with great respect by the large community of nomadic cowherds that moved wherever the pasture was good.

One day a group of cowherds came to Krishna and said, 'Kaliya must be stopped. He has already swallowed three hundred chickens, a hundred and seventy-eight goats, and eighty-three cows. Yesterday he killed the blacksmith's son. This is the last straw. Anyone that tries to cross the river, swim, graze cattle, grow watermelons, milk goats or even walk by the river is in danger. Something must be done.'

Krishna collected a group of brave friends and walked towards the edge of the water. Suddenly a cloud of black smoke rose above the river, shooting flames swirled upwards and, in one quick swipe, Kaliya encircled all of Krishna's friends in the curl of his body and dragged them down to the bottom of the river.

Having done their dirty deed, the five dreaded heads bobbed up again, breaking the surface of the water. This time the Serpent King was floating along casually, mockingly.

Krishna took one flying leap and landed on all of the five hooded heads of the dreaded snake. He crushed one head under one arm and another head under another arm. With his feet he began a heavy-footed dance on the remaining three.

Kaliya felt as if all the mountains of the Himalayas were raining on his head. Such was the power of Krishna's feet.

He decided to dive into his under-water court. He would drown Krishna this way.

Krishna held his breath as Kaliya dived deeper and deeper.

Having killed two of Kaliya's heads Krishna began squeezing the next two under his arms until they also gave up and died.

Madhur Jaffrey

Speak about it

Why is it important to write using paragraphs?
When should you start a new paragraph? Find examples in the passage.

Comprehension

1) What was so strange about Kaliya?

2) Where did he live?

3) What does 'lay waste to the countryside' mean?

4) How old was Krishna? What job did he do?

5) After he had dealt with Krishna's five friends how was the Serpent King behaving?

6) How did Krishna deal with the monster?

Language focus

1) Look through the passage. Decide which paragraphs are there because of a change of time; a change of person; a change of place; a change of topic.

2) Write the topic sentence of this paragraph. List each of the points made to illustrate it.

   Those were the days of boiling hot summers. Our road would be hot, airless and dirty. All the blinds would be down and the curtains closed. The stones on the street would be so hot that you could fry meat, and it was always dusty. Silence hung in the air.

Links to writing

1) These events are not in the right order. Correct the sequence and write the paragraph.

   You knock – old caravan – a storm at night – you go in – you shout – you need shelter – nothing happens – so ... what's in there?

2) Organise and complete the following information to write a story in five paragraphs.

Paragraph	What happens
1	Stormy night – loud crash – wake up – what's happening?
2	Out of bed – downstairs – dark – creaky stairs – afraid
3	Hallway – broken window – no phone line
4	Noise in living room – shadows – heart pounding
5	?

23 Standard English

Read these conversations overheard in the playground.

He ran real quick. They was after him 'cos he was reading one of them books.

I've just ate my tea, but we was out when it happened.

I didn't say nothing to no one. The book what I bought was different.

I never do nothing on Fridays, so the place were dead quiet.

I really likes it when Joshua comes round.

Speak about it

What do you notice about the conversations?

Is there something 'incorrect' about their use of English?

When is it right to use informal English?

When is it not right to use it?

Standard English only came into use when people started to write things down.

Why should this be?

Comprehension

1) These conversations use 'informal English'. Why is this more common in the playground?

2) Can you think of an example when 'formal' English would be better used in the playground?

3) Find an example of when an adjective is used as an adverb (remember most adverbs end in **-ly** and follow verbs).

4) Find an example where the use of a verb is not correct.

5) Find an example of a double negative used in a sentence.

6) Find an example of when 'what' is used instead of 'that'.

Language focus

1) Rewrite what is in the speech bubbles in Standard English to show what is wrong with them.

2) Choose the correct word in each sentence.
   a. I didn't see **(no/any)** snakes.
   b. We painted the picture **(beautifully/lovely)**.
   c. There **(was/were)** two clocks in the market square.
   d. My uncle **(give/gave)** me a new computer for my birthday.
   e. George **(done/did)** his homework at the weekend.
   f. The two dogs **(were/was)** fighting in the street.

3) Rewrite these sentences in Standard English to show what is wrong with them.
   a. 'I ain't done nothing!' shouted the man.
   b. He ran away real quick.
   c. We done the washing-up after lunch.
   d. Them two girls wasn't allowed out to the cinema.
   e. 'He don't know nothing. I already asked him.'
   f. Look in that cupboard what's to your left.
   g. I don't want no trouble from you.

Links to writing

1) Carry out a class survey about the use of informal and Standard English. How many different ways are there of saying **hello**, **goodbye** and **thank you**? Use a chart to gather information.

24 Pronouns

Pronouns can take the place of nouns in sentences.

They are words such as he, she, it **and** their.

They make sentences more interesting. Let's investigate.

The writer of this passage uses the same words over and over again. This makes his writing boring and confusing.

> Fred was given two robots for his birthday. Fred was so excited. Fred wanted to play with his new toys.
>
> The first thing Fred did was to charge up the robot but the robot was broken. Fred went to the other robot and this time the robot sprang into life. Fred was very pleased.
>
> Fred rushed to the office to tell his mother. Fred's mother was not happy to see him. Fred's mother was very busy.

If you use pronouns, it makes it less confusing. The writer does not repeat himself so much.

'He' can replace the noun 'Fred'

'it' can replace the noun 'robot'

> Fred was given two robots for his birthday. **He** was so excited. **He** wanted to play with his new toys.
>
> The first thing Fred did was to charge up the robot but **it** was broken. **He** went to the other robot and this time **it** sprang into life. Fred was very pleased.
>
> Fred rushed to the office to tell his mother. Fred's mother was not happy to see him. **She** was very busy.

'She' can replace the noun mother'

Speak about it

What clues are in the word 'pronoun' that tell you what they do?
What pronouns are used in the passages?
Which nouns do they replace?
Why is the first passage boring?
Do you have to change the sentence in any other way if you use a pronoun?

Comprehension

1) What do pronouns take the place of?

2) How do pronouns stop writers repeating themselves?

3) What would be the effect on the reader if writers did not use pronouns?

4) What sort of noun is replaced by **he** or **she**?

5) What pronouns will you have to use if the noun is in the plural?

Language focus

1) Choose the correct pronouns for these sentences.

   a. Ranjit is very late. Ranjit has been playing with friends. **(she/it/he/her/they)**

   b. Ranjit was playing with his dog and Ranjit was filthy. **(she/it/he/her/they)**

   c. Ranjit's dog was huge. Ranjit's dog was called Rover. **(she/it/he/her/they)**

   d. Ranjit phoned his mum and asked his mum if tea was ready. **(she/it/he/her/they)**

   e. Ranjit's mum called him back. Ranjit's mum was worried. **(she/it/he/her/they)**

2) Choose the correct pronouns to complete these sentences.

   a. **(Us/We)** met the old lady in the supermarket.

   b. **(Him/He)** was more tired than **(us/we)** were.

   c. The teacher liked **(him/he)** more than **(she/her)**.

   d. We listened carefully to **(they/them)**.

Links to writing

1) These sentences can mean more than one thing. The pronouns are not in the right place. Rewrite them correctly.

   a. We met an old man and a little boy whose beard was long and grey. (Clue: who has the beard?)

   b. We have a box for storing cheese that was made two hundred years ago. (Clue: how old is the cheese?)

2) Some pronouns refer to people and things and show things belong to them.

| mine | yours | his | hers | its | ours | theirs |

Write sentences using each of the words in the box, for example. **That scarf is *mine*.**

25 Commas to mark clauses

An **adverbial** is part of a clause. It acts like an adverb and so tells you more about the **verb**, e.g.: **Fred** *went* <u>out to play</u>.

This can be put at the front of a sentence and is called a 'fronted adverbial'. You usually put a comma after a fronted adverbial. <u>**During the afternoon**</u>, we *went* out to play.

Beowulf was an Anglo-Saxon hero. Here is a modern version of one of the fights he had with the monster, Grendel.

From *Dragon Slayer*

In the darkest hour of the spring night Grendel came to Heorot as he had come so many times before, up from his lair and over the high moors, through the mists that seemed to travel with him under the pale moon: Grendel, the Night-Stalker, the Death-Shadow. He came to the foreporch and snuffed about it, and smelled the man-smell, and found that the door which had stood unlatched for him so long was barred and bolted. Snarling in rage that any man should dare to keep him out, he set the flat of his talon-tipped hands against the timbers and burst them in.

Dark as it was, the hall seemed to fill with a monstrous shadow at his coming; a shadow in which Beowulf, half springing up, then holding himself in frozen stillness, could make out no shape nor clear outline save two eyes filled with a wavering greenish flame.

The ghastly corpse-light of his own eyes showed Grendel the shapes of the men as it seemed sleeping, and he did not notice among one of them one who leaned on his elbow. Laughing in his throat, he reached out and grabbed young Hondscio who lay nearest to him, and almost before his victim had time to cry out, tore him limb from limb and drank the warm blood. Then while the young warrior's dying shriek still hung upon the air, he reached for another. But this time his hand was met and seized in a grasp such as he had never felt before; a grasp that had in it the strength of thirty men. And for the first time he who had brought fear to so many caught the taste of it himself, knowing that he had met his match and maybe his master.

Rosemary Sutcliff

Speak about it

What is a clause? Can you find examples in the passage?
Why do you need to use punctuation carefully when you add information with a clause?
How would your reader understand what you have written if you did not use commas properly?

Comprehension

1) What season was it when Grendel attacked?

2) What two names had he been given because of his reputation?

3) Which words tell you that he was angry?

4) What did Beowulf see of Grendel first of all?

5) Find evidence in the passage that Grendel does not care about killing men.

Language focus

1) Add information in the form of clauses to these sentences. Use commas to separate the clause.

   a. I will go out if …

   b. If he had a haircut …

   c. Because I do not understand his language …

   d. After he left the house …

2) You can make sentences more interesting by moving your clauses. Look at the difference between the following two sentences. What changes in the punctuation?

   She will help you if you ask nicely. and **If you ask nicely, she will help you.**

   Do the same with the following.

   a. I phoned the police when I heard the scream.

   b. She must tell her mum if she is nervous.

   c. I travelled by plane although I am afraid of flying.

   d. They do not reply to letters since their office burned down.

   e. I will revise for my exams after I have been to the festival.

3) Write five examples of your own using **although**, **since**, **when**, **if** and **after** and following the same format. Think carefully where to put commas.

Links to writing

1) Continue with the story of Beowulf. What happens to the monster? Does he escape? Does he die? Use the same detailed descriptions. Add information using clauses and phrases to make it more interesting. Think carefully about where to put commas to separate the clauses in the sentences.

26 Time and cause

From *The White Mountains*

**The Tripods have invaded earth!
Henry and Beanpole are trying to
escape from them.**

Seconds later it was in sight, coming
round the base of the hill and,
unmistakably, climbing towards us. It
was some miles away, but coming on
fast – much faster, I thought, than its
usual rate of progress.

Henry said, 'The bushes …'

He did not need to say any more; we were all three running. What he had indicated
offered one of the few bits of cover on the hillside, the only one within reasonable reach.
It was a small thicket of bushes, growing to about shoulder height. We flung ourselves in
amongst them, burrowed into the centre, and crouched down there …

I felt the ground shiver under me, and again and again with still greater force. Then one
of the Tripod's legs plunged across the blue, and I saw the hemisphere, black against the
arc of the sky, and tried to dig myself down into the earth. At that moment the howling
stopped. In the silence, I heard a different, whistling sound of something whipping terribly
fast through the air and glancing fearfully, saw two or three bushes uprooted and tossed
away.

Beside me, Beanpole said: 'It has us. It knows we are here. It can pull the bushes out until
we are plainly seen.'

John Christopher

Speak about it

What is an adverb? Can you find examples in the passage?
What kind of word does an adverb describe?
What is a conjunction? Find examples in the passage.
How do they help to make your sentences longer and more interesting?

Comprehension

1) How far away was the Tripod?

2) Where was the only place to hide?

3) Describe how they tried to hide themselves in the bushes.

4) How can Henry tell that the Tripods were really large from where he was hiding?

5) What words tell you that Henry was looking upwards from the bushes at the Tripod?

6) What was making the 'whistling' sound? What was the Tripod trying to do?

Language focus

1) Identify and list the adverbs used in this passage. Which verbs do they describe? What extra information do they add? How would the meaning be different if you took them away?

2) Adverbs can show how ideas in paragraphs fit together. Use these in sentences.

Adverbs to show 'where'	Here, there, outside
Adverbs to show 'when'	Now, yesterday, later
Adverbs to show 'time'	Often, never, regularly

3) Look carefully at the adverbs in this sentence: 'I heard a different, whistling sound of something whipping terribly fast through the air and glancing fearfully, saw two or three bushes …' If you took them away, what would be missing about your knowledge of the character?

Links to writing

1) Combine these simple sentences to make a more interesting passage. Use conjunctions and then add adverbs to give more detail. Remember, you can change the structure of the sentences to make them more interesting.

The rocket dropped from the clouds. The clouds were thick. They were hovering a few miles from the planet. The rocket gave a jerk. It crashed. It was resting at a dangerous angle over a cliff. Its tail fin was broken.

2) Continue with the story of Henry and Beanpole. How do they escape from the Tripods? Make your sentences longer and more interesting by using suitable conjunctions. When you use a verb, think about whether you can add an adverb to provide extra information about a character or what is happening.

27 Apostrophes for possession

Sporting boo-boos!

At the end of the 1992 FA Cup final, Sunderland, beaten by Liverpool, were mistakenly given the winners' medals and Liverpool were given another team's medals. The players exchanged medals afterwards. The organisers' embarrassment was clear as they apologised publicly.

In 1970, David Webb couldn't collect his medal after scoring the winning goal for Chelsea against Leeds United in the FA Cup final replay at Old Trafford. When the game ended, Webb had swapped shirts with a Leeds player and an official refused to allow him to go up to the directors' box because he thought Webb was a Leeds player (his shirt's colour was obviously wrong). Webb's loss was naturally put right and he was later given his medal in the dressing room.

In September 1997, referee Jeff Arnold was banned for five years by Devon's Amateur Football Association for presiding over a football match that never took place. Mr Arnold wrote a fictitious report on Woodland Fort's 2−0 'victory' over Efford United in the Plymouth and District Combination League's final match of the season. One of the teams had arrived with only four players. The manager's response was to fear a hefty fine if the match didn't take place, so the teams agreed to fake the scoreline. They persuaded Mr Arnold to support them. The ruse proved costly, since both clubs ended up being fined.

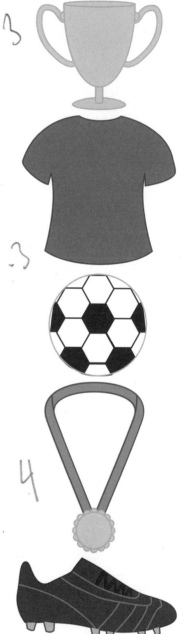

Speak about it

What is an **apostrophe**?
When do you use them to show something belongs to something or somebody? Can you find examples in the passage?
When else do you use them? Find examples in the passage.
Does every word ending in an -s need an apostrophe?

Comprehension

1) Who beat Sunderland in 1992?

2) How do you know the organisers were embarrassed about what had happened at Sunderland?

3) Why couldn't David Webb collect his medal?

4) Where was he given his medal eventually?

5) What does **fictitious** mean? Why did Mr Arnold get into trouble for writing this report?

6) What happened to both clubs?

Language focus

1) List the words containing apostrophes for possession in the passage. Circle where the apostrophe comes.

2) Explain **who** or **what** belongs to **what** or **whom**, e.g. **the winners' medals** (the medals belonging to the winners). Does the position of the apostrophe change?

3) Look at these signs. Explain why the apostrophes are used incorrectly.

a.

b.

c.

d.

Links to writing

1) The following groups of words can change their meaning according to where you place the apostrophe. Write two sentences for each, showing how the meaning can change.

   a. my brothers DVDs

   b. the farmers machinery

   c. the architects plans

   d. his dogs puppies

2) Design and make a poster for your class explaining the rules for using possessive apostrophes. Invent a cartoon character called **Apostrophe Man** to help people to understand. Is there a simple rule to follow? How can you show where best to put apostrophes? What are the mistakes that many people make? Can you think of any mnemonics to help people to learn the correct use?

28 Test your grammar, punctuation and spelling

Grammar

Personal pronouns, possessive pronouns and adverbials

Sort the following under the correct heading.

she   them   ours   swiftly   quite   mine   they

happily   theirs   in addition

(personal) pronoun   possessive pronoun   adverbial

Verb inflections

Finish this chart with the correct verb inflections.

Verb	Present	Past	Present perfect	Present continuous
to make	*I make*	*I made*	*I have made*	*I am making*
to have	he			
to buy	she			
to fall	we			
to travel	they			
to do	you			

Punctuation

Commas with fronted adverbials

Add a comma after the fronted adverbial.

1) In the first instance we must go to collect the car.

2) After we've checked in we can explore the place.

3) In the middle of the night they crept out.

4) Creeping silently and steadily they breathed in the night air.

5) Jumping into the sea they laughed and splashed.

6) Before night fell they were back home safe and sound.

Spelling

Common words

Choose and write out the correct spelling for each one.

Example

grammar   grammer   gramar

1) surprize   suprise   surprise

2) favourite   favorite   faivourite

3) expirience   experience   experiance

4) paragraf   pargraph   paragraph

5) library   librery   libary

6) oposite   opposit   opposite

The suffix /shun/

Use **-tion**, **-sion**, **-ssion** or **-cian** to change these words. Tweak the spelling of the new word if necessary.

1) invent

2) music

3) possess

4) express

5) magic

6) inject

7) extend

8) admit

Glossary

adverbial   a word or a phrase that makes the meaning of a verb more specific

ambiguity   when information is unclear because it can be interpreted in more than one way

analogy   using similarity between two words, e.g. to help you make a decision

bracket   a punctuation mark that is used in pairs to separate or add information (like this)

cohesion   joining information together

cohesive device   a term used to show how the different parts of a text fit together

dash   a punctuation mark that is used – often informally – to add a comment or information in writing. See Punctuation chart

determiner   a determiner modifies a noun, e.g. **the, a, an, this, those, my, your, some, every** or numerals

etymology   a word's history and origin

homophones words that sound the same but have a different meaning and spelling

modal verb   a modal verb changes the meaning of other verbs as it tells us about how certain, able or obliged something or someone is, e.g. **will, would, can, could, may, might, shall, should, must** and **ought**

morphology   considering how a word is made up of different parts

parenthesis   an extra word, clause or sentence inserted into a passage to give non-essential information

possessive pronoun   a word that tells us who owns a noun in a sentence or phrase, e.g. **my, your, his, her, its, our, their, mine, yours, hers, ours, theirs**. They are determiners because they modify the noun

pronoun   a word that is often used instead of a noun or noun phrase,
e.g. **I, you, he, she, it, we, they, this, who**

relative clause   a special type of subordinate clause that makes the meaning
of a noun more specific by using a pronoun to link back to the noun

relative pronoun   we use relative pronouns **after** a noun, to **make it clear**
which person or thing we are talking about or, in relative clauses, to tell us
more about a person or thing, e.g. **who, which, that, who(m), whose**

Punctuation chart

Punctuation mark word	Symbol	Note	Example
apostrophe	'	Can show that something belongs to someone or something	the girl's hat the girls' hats
		Can show that letters are missed out	can't cannot she'd she would/she had
brackets	(....)	Can be used to show that a word or phrase has been added	We said thank you (but we didn't mean it really!).
bullet point	•	Can be used to make a list clear	Things to buy: • sausages • bananas • baked beans
colon	:	Can be used before you make a list	See above
		Can be used to give more examples after the first part of a sentence	The dogs are very funny: they are trained to do tricks.
comma	,	Can make a sentence clear or change the meaning of the sentence	Slow children crossing. Slow, children crossing.
		To separate the items in a list	I like sausages, bananas and baked beans.
dash	–	Can be used to add a bit more information to a sentence It's informal	The dogs are very funny – the old brown one makes me laugh.
full stop	.	Can be used at the end of a sentence to show it has finished	I went to the dog show.
		It also shows that a word is shortened or contracted	On the 23rd of Sept. I went to the dog show.

Handy hints

Spelling

Top tips on spelling

1) Try using your phonics knowledge first.

2) Does it look right? If not, what changes would make sense?

3) Use analogy: do you know another word that sounds similar and that you could use as a starting point, e.g. if it's **baby/babies**, then it's probably going to be **city/cities**.

4) If it's a long word, say the syllables; write each syllable as a chunk.

5) Use morphology: think about the root word and then about whether the word might have a prefix or a suffix that might help you to spell it, e.g. **medical** and **medicine**.

6) Use etymology: think about a word's history and, in particular, its origins in earlier forms of English or other languages to see if that might help you to spell it, e.g. **circumference** from the Latin **circumferentia** meaning the line around a circle.

7) Don't always rely on the spellcheck when working on the computer – keep thinking for yourself so that when you are writing away from technology or on your own, you don't get stuck.

Word lists

Words are taken from word lists which appear in the programmes of study and attainment targets for the new National Curriculum (English).

accidentally	disappear	heart	minute	recent
actually	enough	height	natural	reign
address	exercise	imagine	naughty	remember
believe	extreme	increase	notice	separate
bicycle	famous	island	often	special
breath	favourite	knowledge	opposite	straight
calendar	forward (s)	learn	ordinary	therefore
century	grammar	length	particular	thought
consider	group	library	perhaps	through
describe	guard	material	possible	various
different	heard	mention	quarter	weight

Presentation

Top tips on handwriting

1) Make sure that your pen or pencil is comfortable (and that the pencil is sharp).

2) Use an eraser (rubber, correction fluid or correction pen) if you make a mistake.

3) If you can't read it then others won't be able to!

4) Try to keep it neat all the time.

And ...

Use capital letters for:

- people's names
- people's titles (like **Mrs** Jones)
- places
- days of the week
- months of the year

And ...

Use a full stop at the end of a sentence unless you are using a **?** or a **!**

Rising Stars UK Ltd, 7 Hatchers Mews, Bermondsey Street, London SE1 3GS

www.risingstars-uk.com

Acknowledgements

Page 10 – Extract from Flint by Neil Arskey Copyright – Corgi

Page 14 – Extract from The BFG by Roald Dahl

Page 18 – Extract from *Portrait of the Artist as a Young Dog* by Dylan Thomas, published by Phoenix. Reprinted by permission of David Higham Associates

Page 22 – Extract from *The Warm and the Cold* by Ted Hughes from Season Songs, Faber

Page 24 – 'Pigeons' from *Differences* by Richard Kell, published by Chatto and Windus. Reprinted by permission of The Random House Group Ltd.

Page 28 – Extract from *Shane* by Jack Schaeffer. Reprinted by permission of Don Congdon Associates, Inc. © 1949, renewed by Jack Schaefer.

Page 32 – Extract from 'All Summer in a Day' by Ray Bradbury from *A Medicine for Melancholy* (1959), Doubleday.

Page 34 – 'High' by Walter de la Mare

Page 46 – Extract from 'The Serpent King' by Madhur Jaffrey from *Seasons of Splendour*, Pavilion Books 1985

Page 52 – Extract from *Dragon Slayer* by Rosemary Sutcliff, published by The Bodley Head. Reprinted by permission of David Higham Associates.

Page 54 – Extract from *The White Mountains* (first book in the *Tripods* triology) by John Christopher, published by Hamish Hamilton.

Every effort has been made to trace copyright holders and obtain their permission for the use of copyright materials. The authors and publisher will gladly receive information enabling them to rectify any error or omission in subsequent editions.

All facts are correct at the time of going to press.

Published 2013

Text, design and layout © Rising Stars UK Ltd.

Authors: Les Ray and Gill Budgell

Educational consultant: Shareen Mayers, Routes to Success, Sutton

Text design: Green Desert Ltd

Cover design: West 8 Design

Illustrations: HL Studios

Publisher: Camilla Erskine

Copy Editor: Sarah Davies

British Library Cataloguing in Publication Data.

A CIP record for this book is available from the British Library.

ISBN: 978-0-85769-679-3

Printed by Craft Print International Ltd, Singapore